U. S. MARINE CORPS

CIVIC ACTION EFFORTS IN VIETNAM

MARCH 1965 - MARCH 1966

by

Captain Russel H. Stolfi, USMCR

Historical Branch

G-3 Division

Headquarters, U. S. Marine Corps

1968

PCN 19000412700

A young boy, hopelessly crippled as well as orphaned, receives a ray of happiness from an unusual source. The Marine Corps, a professional combat force, moves in to win the rural population in the ancient game of guerrilla warfare. (photograph courtesy of GySgt Russell W. Savatt)

FOREWORD

The origin of this pamphlet lies in the continuing program at all levels of command to keep Marines informed of the ways of combat and civic action in Vietnam. Not limited in any way to set methods and means, this informational effort spreads across a wide variety of projects, all aimed at making the lessons learned in Vietnam available to the Marine who is fighting there and the Marine who is soon due to take his turn in combat.

Our officers and men in Vietnam are deeply involved in efforts to improve the situation of the Vietnamese people. This pamphlet tells the story of the first formative year of civilian-aid policies, programs, and actions of the III Marine Amphibious Force. To write the study and to perform the extensive and involved research necessary to document its text, the Marine Corps was able to call upon a particularly well-qualified reserve officer, Captain Russel H. Stolfi, who volunteered for several months of active duty in the spring of 1967 for this purpose. In civilian life, Captain Stolfi, who holds a doctor of philosophy degree in history from Stanford University, is Assistant Professor of History at the Naval Postgraduate School, Monterey, California.

The pamphlet is based largely on sources available in the Washington area, including the records of various activities of the Departments of Defense and State, of the CARE organization, and of the Office of the Administrative Assistant to the President. Other sources include correspondence and interviews with participants in the actions described. In some cases documents from which information was taken are still classified, however, the information used in the text is unclassified.

H. NICKERSON, JR.
Major General, U. S. Marine Corps
Assistant Chief of Staff, G-3

REVIEWED AND APPROVED: 9 January 1968

CONTENTS

Foreword		i
Chapter I:	The Changing Pattern of War: Marine Corps Civic Action	1
Chapter II:	The Governing Institutions of the Republic of Vietnam: March 1965-March 1966	4
Chapter III:	Military Civic Action in Vietnam	11
Chapter IV:	The Landing of Major Marine Corps Air and Ground Forces in South Vietnam and the Early Development of Civic Action: March-July 1965	15
Chapter V:	The Turning Point in Civic Action: August 1965	34
Chapter VI:	Accelerating the Pace of Civic Action: The Challenge of support for Rural Construction (September-December 1965)	42
Chapter VII:	A New Calendar Year: Patterns of Civic Action in January-March 1966	61
Notes		82
Appendix	Contents of CARE kits provided through Reserve Civic Actions Fund for Vietnam	96

Chapter I

The Changing Pattern of War: Marine Corps Civic Action

It was early evening and the Viet Cong platoon made its way towards the bridge over the River Phu Bai a few miles southeast of Hue, the former royal capital of Vietnam. Pham Van Thuong, card carrying communist party member and commander of the platoon, could only have felt comfortably at home. He had been born a few miles from his present location. Most of Thuong's short life had been spent close to his birthplace near Hue/Phu Bai where the Marine Corps was now located. Thuong had played, gone to school, and helped his parents in household chores like myriad other children in Vietnam. He had also seen the war against the French, travelled briefly in North Vietnam, and now was participating in a war against a government of his own people in Saigon. Thuong was tough physically and at ease in his early evening environment and revolutionary task. The Viet Cong were rulers of the night. Thuong probably felt little anxiety about the presence of the Popular Forces which had been organized by the local government to resist the Viet Cong. This euphoria was merciful. Pham Van Thuong had only a few more minutes to live.(1)

The Combined Action Company (CAC) ambush had been set carefully and professionally. Marines and Popular Forces had worked together for almost four months in the Hue/Phu Bai area, and the combination of Marine Corps firepower and discipline and Vietnamese familiarity with the terrain had become literally a killing one. At about 2030 on the evening of 29 November 1965, the handful of hunters sensed the presence of the Viet Cong.(2)

Pham Van Thuong possibly never heard the rifle fire which struck him down. No warning had been given. Thuong's final thoughts will never be known. Probably they were the mundane military ones concerning the soundest way to cross the bridge into the hamlet of Phu Bai (VI).(3) Small arms fire from the CAC-3 ambush at the bridge shattered the Viet Cong platoon. Fortune was not with either Thuong or his men. The latter fled southward where they were hit by CAC-4. Then they headed westward into the hills passing through blocking artillery fires on the way. (See Sketch Map).

Since the Marine Corps had formally arrived in Vietnam in March 1965, it had learned a lot about the other war, i.e., the struggle against the clandestine apparatus of the Viet Cong (the Viet Cong infrastructure). This was no surprise because the Marine Corps was a professional military organization which existed to learn swiftly from the shock of combat.

Vietnam was a combat experience that differed little in many of its lessons from other parts of the world; and, Marines had fought and operated in practically all of them. In Vietnam in November 1965, as Thuong's platoon advanced towards the Phu Bai River, the Marine Corps was as confident of producing a professional effort as it had been in Korea during the winter and Guadalcanal in the summer.

But Vietnam offered special frustrations. The original mission, to secure enclaves in the northern region of Vietnam containing air and communications installations, was simplicity itself.(4) The Marine air-ground team promptly occupied those areas and secured them. Equally promptly the Marine Corps leaders sensed the futility of defending a few bits of level terrain to support long-range air bombardment. Under Marine Corps noses the Viet Cong controlled much of the countryside. They had capitalized on the instability of the Vietnamese government from 1963-1965 to push deeply into the lowland and coastal parts of the northern region.(5) Outside of the major cities movement was possible only during daylight, and a sullen, fearful peasantry became omnipresent. When night fell, the forces of the Vietnamese government retracted into various brittle defensive points and the small numbers of hard, well-armed Viet Cong roamed at will.(6)

Targets were available for Marine Corps units in the form of Viet Cong main forces; these were conventionally organized military formations. At carefully selected times the main forces engaged units of both the Army of the Republic of Vietnam (ARVN) and the Marine Corps. But the precious main forces made it a rule to initiate only battles in which success was mathematically predictable. Normally they were beyond knowledge and reach. Furthermore, the destruction of main force units of the Viet Cong yielded little result. Phoenix-like, new forces arose from the ashes of the old. The Viet Cong infrastructure was the life-giver to destroyed units through its ability to recruit from among the peasant masses. At the same time the terroristic apparatus of the infrastructure ensured the neutrality of the Vietnamese peasant. The ultimate enemy of the Vietnamese government and the Marine Corps was everywhere, yet nowhere. The key to the detection of the Viet Cong infrastructure lay in the Vietnamese peasantry, comprising approximately 80 percent of the total population. The peasants alone could eradicate the Viet Cong by exposing their presence and movements to the allied forces. Properly armed and supported, the peasants themselves could destroy the Viet Cong in personal vendettas engendered by the all-pervading form of Viet Cong discipline, terror--the threat and consummation of death sentences against recalcitrant peasants.

Positive security against Viet Cong violence was needed to extract the presence and movements of the rural communist revolutionaries from the uncommitted peasantry. Security in

The concept of the Combined Action Company (CAC) was originated in the Hue/Phu Bai TAOR in August 1965. In this photograph taken on 21 September 1965, 1stLt Paul R. Ek, commander of the original CAC, makes a point with two members of his newly-formed company. (USMC A185800)

Summit conference: the basic unit of the Combined Action Company was the CAC squad. In this photograph, Sgt David W. Sommers (second from right), squad leader and the Marine responsible for the protection of Thuy Tan village in the Hue/Phu Bai TAOR, talks over the report of one of his lance corporals. (USMC A185759)

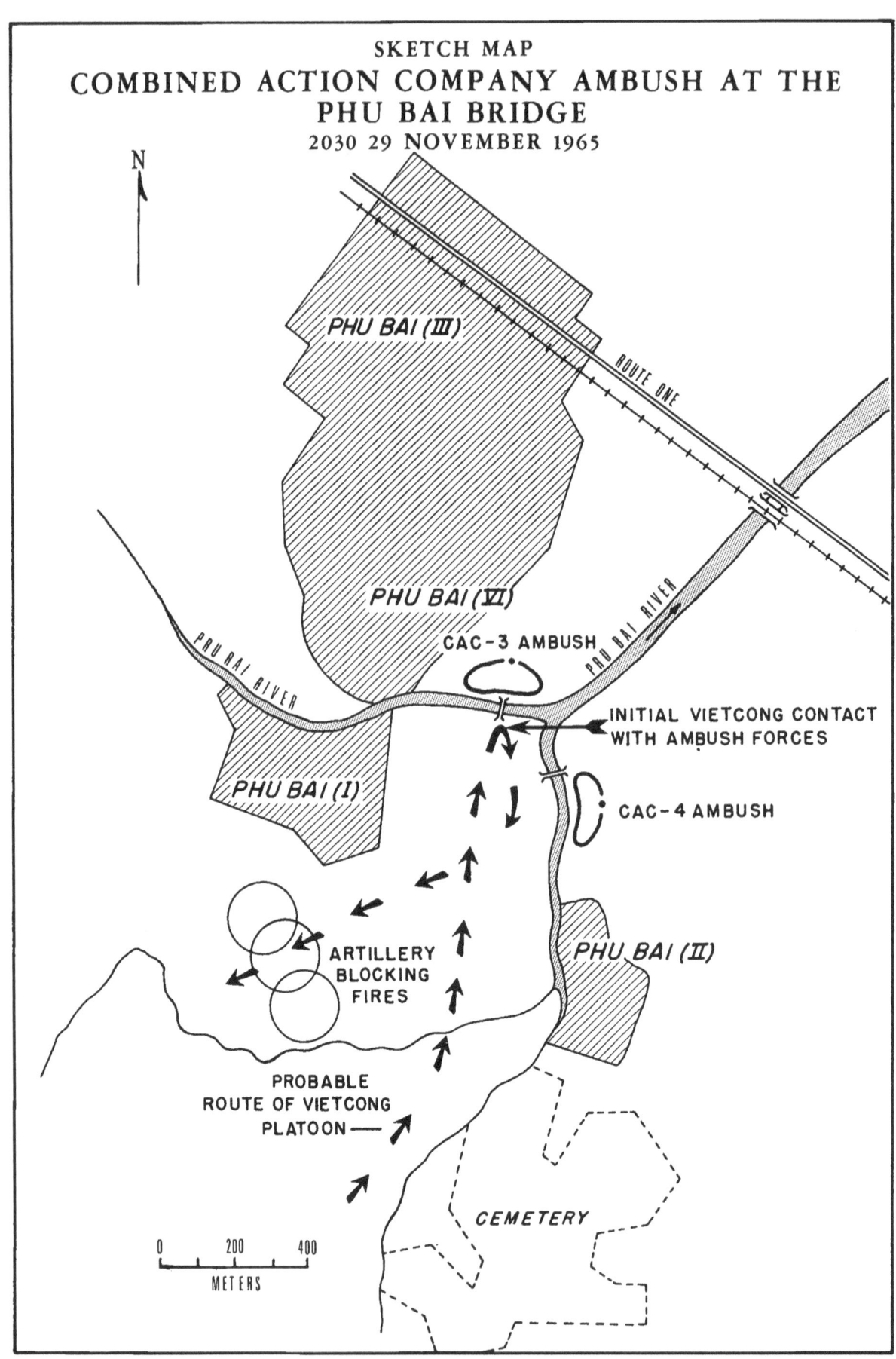

conjunction with an aggressive program of rural development, revolutionary in the sense of its far-reaching and rapid benefits for the peasantry, were the keys to success. Obviously the Marine Corps could not provide security in every village and hamlet. Security and development would rest upon the peasants themselves in conjunction with effective local governing officials. But the Marine Corps could assist in many ways in the reestablishment of security by the Vietnamese government. In one experiment Marine Corps and local rural defense forces, i.e., Popular Forces, recruited and controlled at the village and hamlet level, were formed into CACs whose platoons were to be trained by the Marine Corps to provide 24-hour local security. The CACs were one of many Marine Corps responses to the ultimate problem of reestablishing local government in the hands of the Government of Vietnam (GVN) and freeing the peasants from the Viet Cong terror.(7)

The CAC under the command of First Lieutenant Paul R. Ek was the first of the integrated Vietnamese and Marine Corps defense and training units. The CAC was under the supervision of the 3d Battalion, 4th Marines, and operated in the Hue/Phu Bai enclave southeast of Hue, a city rich in the trappings of Vietnam's historical heritage.(8) Each of its platoons included one Marine Corps rifle squad, and the mission of the Marines was to train the Popular Forces to fight successfully against the Viet Cong anywhere, anytime. In one small way a new wind was blowing through Vietnam.

One of First Lieutenant Ek's squads had been responsible for the successful ambush on 29 November 1965 with its professional request for artillery fire, subsequent coordination with another ambush squad, and the calling of blocking artillery fires (see Sketch Map). The new wind passing through Vietnam carried with it a hardness of will and expertise of operation that would destroy the enemy on his chosen ground-- among the peasantry. Popular Forces would be trained which would be capable of dominating the countryside not only during familiar day but especially during the dreaded night. Behind the screen of effective Popular Forces, expert cadres, i.e., core or nucleus personnel, trained by experts at the national level would destroy the Viet Cong infrastructure. Large units of the Marine Corps and the ARVN would keep at bay and destroy the Viet Cong main force and the Army of North Vietnam. The death of Pham Van Thuong represented something more than an isolated incident. The first fully coordinated effort to defeat the Viet Cong was emerging. Military civic action, expressed in security measures like the CAC concept would provide the link between the war against the enemy main forces and the reestablishment of political control by the GVN at the grass roots level.

Chapter II

The Governing Institutions of the Republic of Vietnam
March 1965 - March 1966

Background

Late in 1955, a national referendum in South Vietnam deposed the head of state, Bao Dai, and chose Prime Minister Ngo Dinh Diem as President of the Republic of Vietnam. By 26 October 1956 a constitution had been promulgated providing for a strong executive, a unicameral national assembly, and a judicial system with safeguards for individual rights. Diem proved to be an effective leader; he was able to consolidate his political position and eliminate the private armies of the religious sects. With U. S. aid he built a formidable national army, established a system of administration, and made progress towards reconstructing the national economy. But Diem's progress threatened North Vietnamese hopes for a unification of the Vietnamese people under northern domination. Simultaneously, Diem's lack of progress in bringing about more rapid social, economic, religious, and political readjustments supported indigenous unrest in the south. Between 1956-1960 the Viet Cong, a melange of northern and southern communists, began and then expanded a campaign to destroy the stability of the southern government and move into the resulting vacuum. By 1960 the control of the movement had slipped decisively into the hands of the Hanoi government because of the stubborn resistance of Diem and his American-supported army and administration.(1)

Between 1960-1963 the Viet Cong movement made crucial gains in South Vietnam. The violent communist tactics of murder and intimidation of the personnel of the Republican government destroyed the government's political apparatus over large parts of rural Vietnam. The Viet Cong occupied the void and using techniques dating back to 1917 established an ominous shadow government which in many rural areas possessed more substance than anything which slain Republican officials could provide. By late 1963, the Diem government, was no longer able to cope with the armed, disciplined, and intellectually coherent movement which threatened its existence. The Vietnamese Army moved inexorably into the position of political power.

During several violent days, 1-4 November 1963, a military coup overthrew the Diem regime, suspended the constitution of 1956, and dissolved the national assembly. The success of the Viet Cong and the agitation of the Buddhists against the Diem Republic had forced a change of government by the armed forces.(2) The revolutionary leaders centralized power in a Revolutionary

Military Council which announced its intention to reinstall civilian leadership as soon as possible. Between November 1963-November 1964 the Vietnamese armed forces split their efforts between political and military operations. The Viet Cong made enormous gains during this period. The temporary nature of the national government weakened the resolve of the governing officials. Simultaneously, the enforced participation of the military leadership in politics restricted effective military operations. By 4 November 1964, civilian leadership had been reintroduced into the government: Tran Van Hung became prime minister and Phan Khac Suu became chief of state. By the turn of 1965, however, Viet Cong gains during the continual progression of temporary national governments ruled out the survival of any democratic, civilian government. The armed forces remained the critical element of stability early in 1965 and forced a readjustment of the civilian government during the period 27 January-16 February 1965.(3) The continuing instability of the government and the concomitant Viet Cong gains forced the intervention of ground combat forces of the United States in March 1965.

The Critical Situation of Early 1965

The U. S. intervention of early 1965 required time for the buildup of significant physical force and even more time for the formulation of an effective program of support for the Government of Vietnam. The Vietnamese political situation continued to deteriorate, and on 11 June 1965 the civilian government, which was unable either to resolve the problem of a new constitution or to cope with the accelerating scale of Viet Cong operations, asked the armed forces to assume the responsibilities of the national government. The armed forces responded by 19 June 1965 with the creation of a Provisional Convention (preliminary constitution) which vested supreme power in a Congress of the Armed Forces. This military government has been called the Ky government because of the position of Air Vice Marshal Nguyen Cao Ky both as prime minister and *de facto* leader of the state.(4)

The Marine Corps arrived in Vietnam under frustrating circumstances. No clear-cut case of foreign aggression was in evidence and the Government of Vietnam in March 1965 was a temporary one which was obviously unable to deal with the revolutionary situation. The Marine Corps found itself in the position of defending an airbase in the Da Nang area in support of an authoritarian civilian government which was soon to be changed to a more authoritarian military government. The enemy, the Viet Cong, was a band of North Vietnamese-influenced communists characterized by an appealing program for change. But the Ky government, the authoritarian military one, made persistent claims that it had no interest in permanent power and the communists proved to be so closely associated with the

Hanoi government that little doubt was left about the unification of the two Vietnams under northern domination in the event of the triumph of the Viet Cong. If the South Vietnamese people had wanted that unification the United States would have had little justification for its intervention in early 1965. But the deliberate attempted murder of the Government of South Vietnam during the period 1959-1965 represented a method of change which was intolerable morally. Finally, the Viet Cong movement was too well organized to pass as a spontaneous rural uprising. Viet Cong brutality and organization were coldly efficient. So much efficiency so close to North Vietnam revealed the threat of the introduction of an ideology detrimental to U. S. interests.

The Formation of a Durable Military Government

The Ky government of June 1965 bore the load of almost ten years of Vietnamese struggle against a calculated attempt to destroy the governments of Vietnam. The government was a last-ditch military one based on the unity of the officer corps of the armed forces. The officer corps provisionally vested the sovereignty of the Vietnamese state in the Congress of the Armed Forces. The executive arm of the Congress was the National Leadership Committee which exercised the powers of the Congress and directed governmental affairs. The Chairman of the National Leadership Committee, who was in effect the head of state, was Lieutenant General Nguyen Van Thieu. Directly below the Leadership Committee was the Central Executive Committee whose chairman was Marshal Ky. He was the central figure in the government and acted as prime minister. Ky had the authority to organize the executive branch of the government and to propose to the Chairman of the National Leadership Committee all cabinet appointments. The center of national power lay ultimately in the National Leadership Committee which was comprised on 19 June 1965 of nine members of the armed forces including Ky as Commissioner for the Executive. Each Corps Commander was represented on the committee also; and, because of the presence of combat soldiers under the Corps Commanders, each commander was a center of armed influence in the state.(5)

The prime minister controlled Vietnam through a cabinet of several ministers and numerous secretaries of state. He appointed and replaced all public officials; approval by the National Leadership Committee was required only in the case of Province Chief, Director General, or higher. Mayors of the autonomous cities and the Prefecture of Saigon were also appointed by the prime minister. Below the national level a vast hierarchy of local government existed. Four Corps Areas or Regions existed in which the senior governmental delegate was the military commander. The Commanding General, III Marine Amphibious Force, became the senior military advisor to the

Vietnamese general commanding I Corps (the First Region) in August 1965. Subordinate to the Vietnamese Corps Commanders were the Provincial Chiefs who directed the efforts of the District Chiefs and carried out the functions of government at the provincial level. The Province Chiefs, who were advised by elected Provincial Councils, provided extensive services for the Vietnamese people and were supported by technical assistants from the national ministeries. Below the provinces (43 in number) were ranged districts (234), grouped villages (2558), and hamlets (13,211). Most of the population of Vietnam was rural and resided in the hamlets. The national government ultimately contacted most of the population at the hamlet level, i.e., the grouped villages were units of administrative convenience and were comprised of a certain number of hamlets, usually four to six.(6)

The Viet Cong

The Viet Cong had concentrated their attack on the Government of Vietnam by destroying the governing officials at the hamlet and village levels. The Viet Cong emphasized the political aspects of the struggle and replaced slain, kidnapped, and terrorized officials with communist or communist-appointed officials. The communists formed a government within a government and literally stole the bodies and minds of the peasants by a combination of armed force and astute rural propaganda. But the appeal to force is central in the Viet Cong movement and has remained, in combination with superlative organization, the main strength of the movement. The following comment illustrated the strength of the Viet Cong appeal to the peasantry but also revealed striking weaknesses. A village elder characterized their rule by saying:

> If you do as the Viet Cong say they are very correct.
> They never steal. They tax.
> If they take a chicken they pay.
> If you do not cooperate, they shoot you in the stomach.(7)

The Viet Cong generated much fear amongst the rural population of South Vietnam by their policy of balanced ruthlessness. In areas where the Government of Vietnam was unable to provide security for its citizens, the Viet Cong were able to swim undetected in a sea of terrorized humanity. Simultaneously, the Viet Cong made exaggerated promises of a better life for the Vietnamese peasant. Government projects were ridiculed, harassed, and destroyed by the rural Robin Hoods who had to produce no results until they were in power. The Viet Cong used promises of a better future with the reality of present violence to erode the influence of the Republican government. The Republic could succeed against the movement only by the implementation of a more effective program designed to win back the fearful rural masses. The harsh geographical reality of a hostile border abutting on Vietnam in the North made the chances of unsupported government success against the Viet Cong problematical.(8)

Vietnamese Rural Construction (1965) and Revolutionary Development (1966)

In 1965 with disaster staring it in the face, the Vietnamese government, with the urging of the U. S. Mission Council in Vietnam, executed a well-conceived rural pacification plan. Improved civil/military coordination was achieved and significant changes in terminology were made during the year. For example, on 5 April 1965 the government supplanted the term pacification with the new one, rural construction. But the instability of the government during the first half of 1965 slowed the release of funds for the rural construction program. The national government did not release monies until April 1965, and the program was further slowed by changes in the national organization for rural construction and finally the death of the Minister of Rural Construction in August 1965. As a result, the government's accomplishments in rural construction in 1965 were slight. But the combination of the Ky military government and massive U. S. ground and air forces prevented decisive Viet Cong success even though the allies produced no forward momentum of their own.(9)

Prime Minister Ky initiated planning for 1966 rural construction in September 1965 when he requested that the U. S. Mission Liaison Group help to determine the National Priority Areas for Rural Construction in 1966. The reason for the establishment of those areas was to ensure the concentration of national resources in vital areas of the country. The government established four priority areas for the calendar year 1966. The area around Da Nang, Quang Nam Province, became one of them.(10)

Planning continued in November and December 1965 and on 15 December 1965, the Vietnamese Joint General Staff published Directive AB 140 as the basic military plan for support of rural construction in 1966. The directive assigned Corps Priority Areas in addition to the national areas and directed the holders of real power in Vietnam, the Corps Commanders, to support rural construction in their areas. The combined campaign for 1966 was published by the U. S. Military Assistance Command and the Vietnamese Joint General Staff on 31 December 1965 and linked the U. S. and Vietnamese military plans with rural construction. But progress was slow in 1966. Civilian rural construction activities suffered from the lack of trained cadres, i.e., organizing personnel, to provide the leadership at the hamlet level for the reestablishment of government control. But the government continued to press for rural improvement and its determination was revealed in the change of the term rural construction to the more forceful expression, revolutionary development. With the graduation of the first revolutionary development cadres in May 1966, and the aggressive leadership of the Minister of Revolutionary Development, the government's program began to edge forward after the middle of 1966. Military activities proved to be the vital flaw in the revolutionary development program. The government planners had not given enough firm and precise direction to the armed forces regarding their role. The Vietnamese armed forces continued to carry out the task of combatting the main force of the Viet Cong and failed to provide the security required to ensure the success of the revolutionary development groups. Security devolved on the Regional and Popular Forces; but, they remained too weak to provide adequate security without substantial reinforcement by the Vietnamese army.

Rural construction had become by December 1965 the thread which productively held together the military and the civil efforts of the Republic. The plans for rural construction not only coordinated the Republican military and civil activities but also related them to the U. S. and Free World military, political, and humanitarian aid programs. Rural construction became the government's coordinated plan for survival. No Ministry of Rural Construction existed in Vietnam throughout 1965. By 12 October 1965, however, a Secretary of State for Rural Construction had been created and Aspirant General Nguyen Duc Thang became first holder of the position. Later, in the national government's reorganization of 21 February 1966, General Thang became Secretary of State for Revolutionary Development within the Ministry of War and Construction. By July 1966, however, Thang had become Minister of Revolutionary Development with two secretaries of state operating under his direction.(11)

Rural construction evolved from late 1965 onwards as the attempt of the national government to reestablish its control over the basic, traditional Vietnamese political groupment--the hamlet. Hamlets had been part of Vietnamese peasant life for over two millenniums; they were political bedrock for the Vietnamese nation. The importance of the hamlet was shown in the late 1940's when the Viet Minh, rural revolutionaries extraordinary, were forced to create the grouped village, an administrative superstructure used to control the hamlets. But the grouped village existed in Vietnam only insofar as it was comprised of a certain number of hamlets. The war has been fought around the latter which have borne the brunt of destruction. General Thang, with a keen sense of historical reality, recognized their importance for both sides in the present struggle. He designed the revolutionary development program to rebuild the basic structure of traditional Vietnamese life and at the same time bring about beneficial change in the life of the Vietnamese peasant.(12)

The spearhead of the rural construction program had been the People's Action Teams (PATs), 40-man groups which began the process of political and social change in secured areas. At the end of 1965 the Vietnamese began to train more effective personnel called Revolutionary Development Cadre (RD Cadre) who were organized into 59-man Revolutionary Development Groups (RD Groups). General Thang's most important task, outside of coordinating the support of the Vietnamese and the U. S. governments behind revolutionary development, has been the training of the young men who would drive the program into the political and social foundation of Vietnam. The battlefield of the struggle for change in 1965 and 1966 was in the areas where the PATs and later the RD Groups were committed. The Marine Corps quickly sensed the importance of revolutionary development and by the turn of 1966 emphasized civic action and psychological warfare in direct support of revolutionary development.

Chapter III

Military Civic Action in Vietnam

Military civic action is something which used the formidable potential of armed and disciplined military organizations to accomplish difficult civil tasks. History had shown that men could do anything with bayonets except sit on them, and this general notice was well taken in the case of Vietnam.(1) In Vietnam, sitting on bayonets in the 1960s would have been using the Allied armed forces only for large unit actions against the elusive main forces of the Viet Cong. But had the Allies followed that course of action, the struggle for control of the Vietnamese peasantry by the GVN would have remained unaffected because the Viet Cong infrastructure would have been more than a match for the local Vietnamese government. The Allied armed forces were the most effective organizations for the supression of the guerrilla terror and had to be used in a concept which was balanced between combat against the main forces of the Viet Cong and security for local government.

Well before intervening with major ground forces at the request of the GVN in 1965, the U. S. Government had realized the importance of military organizations in accomplishing beneficial change in countries which were modernizing themselves. By 1962, "U. S. military and assistance legislation and directives provide/ d / that military assistance programs should encourage the use of local military and paramilitary forces in developing countries on projects helpful to social and economic development."(2) The U. S. Government encouraged the use of the ARVN for operations in support of pacification. But the ARVN operations were weakly developed because of the expressed view that economic and social aid by the armed forces should not "detract from capabilities to perform primary military missions."(3)

Operations against the main force of the Viet Cong, however, were only one part of the ARVN struggle to support the central objective of the war in Vietnam. That objective--the creation of a Government of the Republic of Vietnam viable enough to crush the insurgency and to resist future aggression--was too difficult to tie up the ARVN simply in the defense of fixed installations and actions against the main force of the Viet Cong. In the existing war the immediate objective was to create a civilian population confident enough of the protection of the GVN to expose the presence and movements of the insurgents. The central reality of the war was a Vietnamese population which was overwhelmingly rural. As a result, both the ARVN and the Marine Corps had to support local, rural government scattered through myriad hamlets and connected by a primitive communications network. Marine Corps support, for example, had to range far beyond the static defense of air installations.

Rural Construction

The Marine Corps, however, was an organization which did not exist to create a program for viable government in a foreign state. That program lay with the GVN, and existed in spite of the dislocation of 1963-1965. In 1965, rural construction was the term describing the government's program to secure the central objective of the war.(4) The government's plan was a sound one which concentrated on the central reality of life in the new state--a primitive, rural way of existence.(5) The program was of paramount importance to the Marine Corps. Success of the program promised victory over the Viet Cong, stability for the Republic, and the release of U. S. military forces. The rural construction program was comprised of:

> The integrated military and civil process to restore, consolidate, and expand governmental control so that nation building /could/ progress throughout the Republic of Vietnam. It consist/ed/ of those coordinated military and civil actions to liberate the people from VC control, restore public security, initiate political and economic development, extend effective government authority and win the willing support of the people towards those ends.(6)

The definition was dry but the program was important. How was military civic action related to rural construction? Civic action was largely the friendly military plan of support for rural construction. It existed in close coordination with large and small unit combat operations against the Viet Cong. Military civic action in March 1965 was by theoretical definition primarily a function of the ARVN. But no directives existed discouraging U. S. military participation in civic action; to the contrary, U. S. military forces were encouraged to participate. The following Marine Corps definition of military civic action concentrates on the role of the indigenous armed forces in the support of government but it also ties in the efforts of U. S. forces:

> The use of preponderantly indigenous military forces on projects useful to the local population at all levels in fields such as education, training, public works, agriculture, transportation, communications, health, sanitation, and other contributing to economic and social development, which would also serve to improve the standing of the military forces with the population (U. S. forces may at /any time/ advise or engage in military civic actions in overseas areas).(7)

Combined Action Companies had two missions. The first was that of providing security for Vietnamese peasants. The second, shown here, was the encouraging of self-help projects among the villagers. In this scene Cpl Earl J. Suter helps to build a shelter for his CAC squad at Thuy Luong two miles south of Hue/Phu Bai on 25 September 1965. (USMC A185707)

Food for the needy: the distribution of food began to reach major proportions by the end of 1965. In this photograph taken at Tra Kieu near Da Nang on 17 August 1965, two officers of MAG-16 present supplies received from the U.S. Agency for International Development to the village priest for distribution to the local orphanage and old people's home. (USMC A184979)

This general definition was valid for the military organizations of states throughout the world in the process of peaceful technical change. But the definition was not precise enough for the Vietnamese situation. In Vietnam, military civic action served to link together the formal combat effort of the military forces with the political, social, and economic reconstruction efforts of the GVN. Civic action harnessed energies of both the ARVN and the Marine Corps, which remained after the formal combat commitments, to the tasks of rural construction.

The Place of Marine Corps Civic Action in the Vietnamese War

The question then arose: where did Marine Corps civic action fit in with the overall struggle in Vietnam? This question had to be answered before the civic actions of the Marine Corps could have real meaning. Chart Number One presents the situation graphically. The total Marine Corps effort in the triple sense of large unit, counterguerrilla, and civic actions was part of a larger effort to control and reconstruct Vietnam and to defeat the Viet Cong. The Commanding General, III Marine Amphibious Force (CG, III MAF) was highly placed in the U. S. chain of military command and after August 1965, he functioned as Senior Military Advisor to the Vietnamese general commanding the First Military Region. Additionally, the CG, III MAF, coordinated his operations with the programs of the various U. S. Government agencies and departments. The Vietnamese political effort was controlled by the general commanding the First Military Region; but that effort functioned largely through the local civilian officials who were supported technically by the national ministries.(8)

Marine Corps civic action also had to be set in the political context of U. S. involvement in a revolutionary situation in a sovereign state.(9) The basic premise of U. S. involvement was the protection of U. S. and Free World interests in SE Asia. These interests were best served by the support of the existing Government of Vietnam. But because of the political sovereignty of Vietnam, U. S. support for the Vietnamese government had to take the form of support for that government's chosen plan for survival. For example, large unit ground actions by the Marine Corps were ultimately effective only if they reinforced the stability of the South Vietnamese government and advanced its survival plan.

The Coordination of Civic Action and Vietnamese Plans for Survival

Marine Corps civic action had to be coordinated with all of the activities supporting Vietnamese revolutionary development and had to take into account the total availability of resources to be really effective.(10) For example, Marine assistance in the construction of a hamlet schoolhouse was a frustrating event for the local population and the Marine Corps alike if no teachers were available to grace the school. The Marine Corps was unable to create Vietnamese teachers, and the local hamlet or village government was also unable to manufacture them. Coordination with the higher levels of government concerning the availability of both human and material resources was one of the keys to success. Generally the Marine Corps had to coordinate with the following general entities: (1) the Vietnamese government (district, provincial, regional levels), (2) U. S. Government agencies and departments, and (3) private U. S. relief organizations. Coordination was mandatory if any lasting effect were to be obtained from civic action. It was probably accurate to say that effective Marine Corps civic action began with Major General Lewis W. Walt's formation in August 1965 of a Joint Coordinating Council for the I Corps Tactical Zone (ICTZ). General Walt, who had become commanding general of the III Marine Amphibious Force (III MAF) in June 1965, was aware of the immense process of historical change taking place in Vietnam and was determined to join that process and reinforce in a direction favorable to the Vietnamese government.(11)

The direction which was sensed by him as being decisive in midsummer 1965 was support of Vietnamese rural construction. By August 1965, with his appointment as Senior Military Advisor to the Commanding General, I Corps, General Walt began to implement a coordinated civic action program with the formation of a council which would include representatives of all of the organizations in the I Corps Tactical Zone supporting rural construction. The purpose of the council was to coordinate the services and resources of all organizations, military, civilian and private, in support of rural construction. The thread which began to run through Marine Corps civic action after August 1965 was that of self-effacing support for Vietnamese rural construction.

CHART NUMBER ONE
US/GVN REVOLUTIONARY DEVELOPMENT STRUCTURE - MARCH 1966

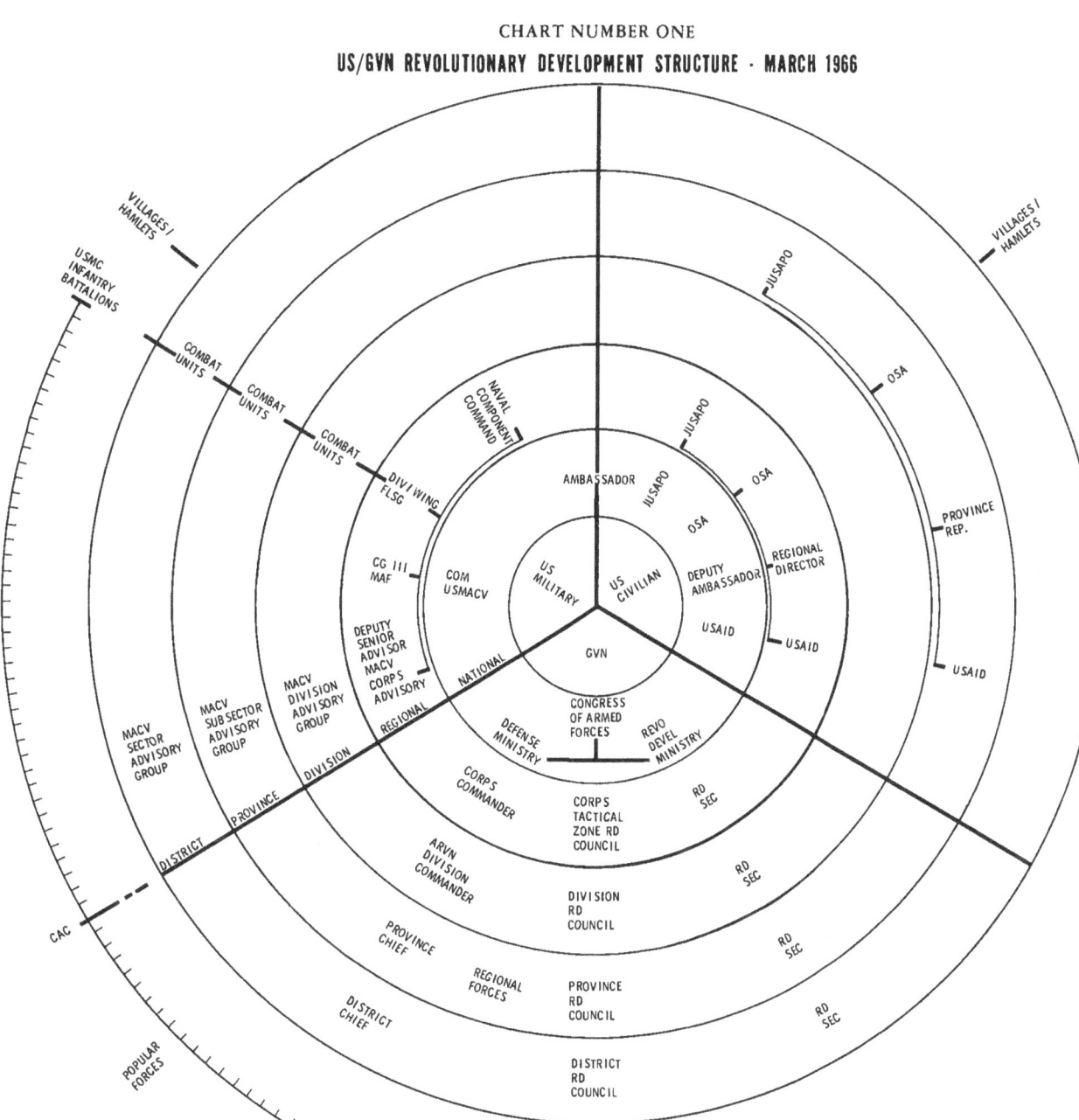

Chapter IV

The Landing of Major Marine Corps Air and Ground Forces in South Vietnam and the Early Development of Civic Action: March-July 1965

Background

By March 1964, the United States Government realized that its hopes of an early ending to the conflict in South Vietnam were premature. General Maxwell D. Taylor, Chairman of the Joint Chiefs of Staff, stated that the Viet Cong had taken advantage of the instability of the Vietnamese Government and the lack of coordination and diffusion in the strategic hamlet program (the forerunner of revolutionary development) to make vast gains.(1) The Viet Cong had negated the strategic hamlet operations and had passed over to the offensive, launching major daylight attacks against the ARVN. The situation was plainly deteriorating and by the end of 1964 the U. S. advisory effort was built up to a total of 20,000 personnel. The situation in Southeast Asia had deteriorated in other ways also. Various ties had existed between the Viet Cong and the Democratic Republic of North Vietnam since the beginning of the struggle in 1956; but, in 1964 North Vietnamese assistance had become concrete in the form of massive infiltration by the North Vietnamese Army into the south. A precarious balance, at best, had existed in South Vietnam late in 1963. By late 1964, North Vietnamese intervention and the gains of the Viet Cong in combination with the internal instability in the south, threatened to destroy the balance.(2)

At the turn of 1965, the Viet Cong supported by elements of the North Vietnamese Army including the major part of the 325th Division maintained heavy military pressure against the GVN. The full measure of Viet Cong confidence was revealed in the impolitic attack on the U. S. military compound at Pleiku. The Viet Cong, for whom the essence of the struggle was political, took leave of sound political judgement in creating the incident. President Lyndon B. Johnson had made it clear that the communist tactics of force and intimidation against the GVN were not an acceptable means of social and economic change even though change was the common goal of both the United States and the two Vietnams. The attack at Pleiku focused violence against the U. S. Government, furnished stark evidence of the method of advance by force, and resulted in a reaction so powerful that the heady smell of communist victory turned to one of aid-station antiseptic. Roses turned to iodine as the Viet Cong realized that force indeed was the ultimate arbitrator in the world of competing sovereign states.

The Landing of Major Marine Combat Forces

The United States began to bomb "selected" targets in North Vietnam in February 1965, and under the pressure of bold Viet Cong advances, sent the first major ground combatant forces into the Republic. Early on Monday morning 8 March 1965, Marines under the direction of the Headquarters, 9th Marine Expeditionary Brigade (MEB) landed by sea and air close to Da Nang, Quang Nam Province, Republic of Vietnam. Although the intervention of ground forces ultimately ensured the survival of the Republic, the immediate physical effect on military operations in Vietnam was negligible. Brigadier General Frederick C. Karch, Commanding General, 9th MEB had only two battalion landing teams (BLTs) under his command with supporting and reinforcing air, artillery, antiaircraft, engineer, and logistics organizations. The most significant factor, though, which restricted Marine Corps operations was the Vietnamese government's fear concerning its own sovereignty. The 9th MEB was originally restricted to a few square miles of territory in several different locations. The locations became known as Tactical Areas of Responsibility (TAORs) and the Vietnamese restricted Marine Corps operations to those areas. The mission of the 9th MEB was strictly defensive--to secure the Da Nang Airbase. And the defense, in deference to the wishes of the Vietnamese government was to extend no farther than the tight limits of the assigned TAORs.(3)

Neither the national nor the local Vietnamese government was able to predict the reaction of the populace to the Marine Corps--a foreign ground combat force. The inpredictability of the civilian reaction forced a gradualist approach on the GVN. The government isolated the Marines first within the perimeter of the uninhabited airbase and then to Hills 327 and 268 (heights in meters) immediately west of the base. The hills were also practically uninhabited.(4) The TAOR, which was physically divided into two parts, had an area of only eight square miles and included the sparse population of 1,930 civilians. The Marines outnumbered the civilian population within the TAOR and remained sealed off from the rest of the people. The Marines were separated psychologically from the people by the limited defensive mission and physically by wire obstacles and cleared fields of fire.(5)

The Beginnings of Marine Corps Civic Action

Marine Corps civic action during the period 8 March-20 April 1965 was sharply restricted by the Marine Corps isolation. Civic action consisted primarily of spontaneous acts of commiseration and charity by individual Marines towards a small population whose pacification was largely extraneous to the tightly circumscribed Marine Corps mission. The concept of purposeful Marine Corps civic action to support the GVN was absent during March 1965 and most of April. The 9th MEB was keenly aware of the importance of popularizing the presence of Marines in Vietnam but with the continuing buildup and the emphasis on static positions in the absence of room for maneuver, neither the need nor the opportunity for civic action arose. Marine Corps efforts to popularize the presence of the 9th MEB could be characterized by the words limited people-to-people contact. No full-time Civil Affairs Officers existed at battalion or squadron level. And the Civil Affairs Officers at brigade level, and after 15 April 1965, with the 3d Marines, were simply not in the mainstream of concern in March and April 1965. The Marine Corps was busy getting ashore. And during the first two months, "ashore" was a humble area divorced from the great struggle for the loyalty of the Vietnamese people.(6)

The Vietnamese government was only gradually relieved of its nervousness about the presence of Marines. By early April 1965, however, the general indifference of the civilian population to the Marine Corps landing was apparent. The care taken by the Marine Corps to reduce friction between Marines and Vietnamese civilians made a favorable impression which was reinforced by the embryonic but positive and sincere efforts of the individual Marine to relieve misery wherever it was present. At the same time it became apparent that the Marine Corps needed to establish control over areas well beyond the fixed perimeter of the Da Nang Airbase to ensure its security. On 20 April 1965, after discussion and coordination between the CG, 9th MEB and the CG, ICTZ, the Marine Corps began to patrol forward in its TAORs beyond the wire and other obstacles of the static positions. Soldiers and civil affairs personnel of the ARVN accompanied the Marine patrols which were intended to make the local villagers aware of the presence of the Marine Corps and to allow the Marines to meet the local governing officials on a face-to-face basis.(7)

On 10 April 1965, several days prior to the time that units of the 9th MEB began to patrol forward in their TAORs, the Da Nang area of responsibility was expanded from eight to twelve square miles. Although the total area of responsibility remained small, the population jumped several hundred percent to the substantial total of 11,441 civilians. On the same day, the number of BLTs in Vietnam rose from two to three with the arrival of BLT 2/3, i.e., the BLT formed around the 2d Battalion, 3d Marines. One day later, elements of that organization were lifted by helicopter to the village of Hue/Phu Bai (see Map Number Three) with the mission of temporarily securing the airfield and the radio station located there. On 14-15 April 1965, the strength of the 9th MEB rose to a total of four BLTs with the arrival of BLT 3/4. This combat organization was committed in the Hue/Bhu Bai area and relieved the units which had temporarily secured the air and radio installations. The two additional battalions accentuated the lack of room for maneuver for the Marine Corps units within the enlarged but still sharply restricted TAORs.(8)

Summary: March-April 1965

The Marine Corps carried out a combat mission in March 1965 which entailed an extensive buildup of strength and the simultaneous orientation to the realities of war in Vietnam. The initial problems of building from a void in ground combat strength at the water's (and airfield's) edge to strength capable of carrying out the assigned mission were those simply of getting ashore. Although the landing was unopposed and several hundred Marines had been ashore in various missions prior to the landing of the 9th MEB, the task demanded the full concentration of the Headquarters, 9th MEB, and the maneuver and supporting elements.

The strictly circumscribed mission of the Marine Corps and the low population of the operating areas limited contact with the civilian population. Both the mission and the operating areas permitted by the sovereign Republic of Vietnam reflected profound fear of U. S. military strength. The Republic had no way of gauging the reaction of a restless, war-weary peasantry to the intrusion of an obviously foreign, e.g., caucasian/negro, ground force. The ARVN, which had become partly separated from the population through its emphasis on operations against the main force of the Viet Cong, did not offer a comforting precedent for the arrival of a new military force in the country. The Republican government and the ARVN expected and were prepared for difficulty and reduced the contact between Marines and the peasantry to a minimum. The Marine Corps preoccupation with the buildup of strength and the Vietnamese concern over protecting the sovereignty of the Republic permitted only a moderate amount of spontaneous civic action and practically no well-organized activity in March-April 1965.

The Expanding Marine Corps Effort:
Formation of the III Marine Amphibious Force

Late in April 1965 the decision was made to establish a new TAOR for the Marine Corps which would include the area eventually known as Chu Lai, a sandy uncultivated waste near An Tan, Quang Tin Province, lying approximately 75 miles southeast of Da Nang by road. The Marine Corps chose this uninhabited area for use as an airbase for Marine Corps fighter and attack aircraft and a center for the support of the GVN in the nearby heavily populated coastal areas of Northern Quang Ngai Province and Central Quang Tin.(9) To secure the Chu Lai area the Marine Corps had to commit a force substantial enough to move the center of gravity of the 3d Marine Division from Okinawa to the Republic of Vietnam. The results of the commitment of the 3d Marine Expeditionary Brigade at Chu Lai on 7 May 1965 were

far-reaching. The place of the division commander was in
Vietnam with the bulk of his division. The Marine Corps concept
of the air-ground team also required the presence of an equivalent air element. In a swift rush of events, the HQ, III MEF
a command element senior enough to control a division-wing
organization, established itself ashore at Da Nang at 0800,
6 May 1965. Almost simultaneously the Headquarters, 3d Marine
Division (-) (Reinforced) (Forward) arrived and was activated
at Da Nang. One day later on 7 May 1965, III Marine Expeditionary Force was redesignated III Marine Amphibious Force (III MAF)
for political reasons. The word, expeditionary, smacked too
much of the gunboat imperialism of a bygone era and had been
used by the French forces which entered Vietnam at the end of
the Second World War. Less than one week later the Headquarters,
1st Marine Air Wing (MAW) (Advanced) was established at the
Da Nang Airbase. On 12 May 1965, when the Chu Lai amphibious
operation terminated, command of all of the Marine Corps
landing force elements in Vietnam passed to the CG, III MAF.(10)

The massive buildup of early May shifted the Marine Corps
mission away from a tightly circumscribed defensive one. By
12 May 1965, seven battalions stood in Vietnam and were deployed
within three TAORs totalling the modest area of 15 square
miles. The battalions were more than capable of defending
their assigned areas. Therein lay the inefficiency of the
situation. They had the mobility, firepower, and numbers to
keep the Viet Cong at far greater distances than those involved
in holding 15 square miles. Additionally, the presence of the
Viet Cong infrastructure became familiar to Marines as an enemy
closer and more real than the main force of the Viet Cong. III
MAF required room for offensive maneuver forward of the tight
perimeters which had been established around the airfields and
radio installations. And the GVN needed the security that the
Marine Corps combat units could provide in support of rural
construction and the offensive strength which could be used
against the main force of the Viet Cong. The situation in
which more than 14,000 Marines were defending several square
miles containing approximately 14,000 civilians was untenable
in the light of the desperate situation of the GVN.

In May 1965, a civic action effort began which was advanced
beyond the stage of spontaneous people-to-people contact between
Marines and Vietnamese civilians. Between 4-10 May 1965, BLT
2/3, which was assigned the TAOR northwest of Da Nang, cleared
the village of Le My (also known as Hoa Loc) (see Map Number
One) For the following reason, however, the experience was a
frustrating one which served to introduce more advanced Marine
Corps civic action into Vietnam. Lieutenant Colonel David A.
Clement, Commanding Officer, 2d Battalion, 3d Marines, who had
cooperated closely with the Chief of the Hoa Vang District
during the clearing operation, realized almost instinctively
that his strenuous efforts would be negated unless continuing
pressure was brought to bear on the remnants of the Viet Cong

infrastructure in Le My village. Accordingly, the first complete pacification in which Marines were involved began in earnest on 11 May 1965 after the elimination of most of the Viet Cong from Le My.(11)

Farther south in the TAOR located at Chu Lai, the arrival of a third BLT on 12 May 1965 gave the Marine Corps a chance to conduct offensive action in support of Vietnamese rural construction. The airfield which was being constructed at Chu Lai from Airfield Matting, AM2 (aluminum alloy material), was located only a few hundred meters from the South China Sea. The perimeter was unusually easy to defend with one side being close to the sea, the immediate area uninhabited, and the general area sparsely peopled. As a result, the three BLTs were more than adequate for the defense and were able to conduct offensive operations both along the coast and inland.

Effective 25 May 1965, the GVN authorized the first major expansion of the Marine Corps TAORs. Until that date the Marine Corps landing force had been literally bulging out of its operating areas especially in the Chu Lai area. The Da Nang TAOR was expanded to the impressive total of 156 square miles and included a civilian population of 46,146 persons. The GVN also expanded the Chu Lai and the Hue/Phu Bai TAORs, and the Marine Corps became responsible for the protection of a total area of 239 square miles with a civilian population of approximately 77,000 persons.(12) In the Chu Lai area, favorable opportunities arose for civic action, and the 4th Regimental Landing Team (redesignated on 12 May 1965 as 4th Marines) produced results on the basis of local initiative. The 4th Marines directed its efforts towards building civilian confidence in the Marine Corps and acquiring intelligence about the Viet Cong.

Advancing Concepts of Civic Action: May-June 1965

Early in May 1965, the Civil Affairs Officer of III MAF, Major Charles J Keever, had arrived in Vietnam and had proposed a concept for civic action. Additionally, he began to write instructions for the reporting of civic action activities. But coordination with the U. S. and Vietnamese government agencies and the U S private relief organizations in order to formulate an effective civic action program was a time consuming task. The Civil Affairs Officer made staff visits in the Chu Lai and Da Nang areas to get information about the Vietnamese people and the details of their home life as well as the civic action activities of the Marine Corps combat and supporting units. HQ, III MAF greatly expanded its functions of coordination within its TAORs as a result of the Letter of Instruction of 29 May 1965 from the Commander, U. S. Military Advisory Command, Vietnam (ComUSMACV), appointing the CG, III MAF, as Special Area Coordinator for the Da Nang area. The CG,

III MAF, became responsible for liaison with local military and civilian leaders concerning matters involving U. S. military personnel.(13) By the end of May, the Civil Affairs Officer of III MAF was functioning within a large area permeated by the clandestine Viet Cong political apparatus. The Marine Corps began to rub shoulders with the Viet Cong infrastructure and the friction which was created helped to impress on HQ, III MAF, the importance of Vietnamese rural construction. The CG, III MAF, and his Civil Affairs Officer (CAO) began to realize the importance of directing Marine Corps civic action towards support of the governing officials of the Republic and the Vietnamese program of rural construction.

On 7 June 1965, HQ, III MAF, now under the leadership of Major General Lewis W. Walt, promulgated concepts of civic action for the Republic of Vietnam.(14) General Walt had arrived in Vietnam on 30 May 1965 and had assumed command of III MAF on 4 June 1965 from Major General William R. Collins. As events would show, he was extraordinarily interested in supporting Vietnamese plans for rural construction. The instructions issued under his authority proved unusually durable. HQ, III MAF, correctly identified the government's rural problems and began to establish the mission and the concept of operations to assist the Republic in overcoming the attack on its authority.(15) The order of III MAF left little doubt that civic action in support of the hard pressed local government and not "civil affairs/military government operations as that term is normally understood" would be the basis of Marine Corps action.(16) The spirit came out strongly in the following part of the concept of operations:

> Civic action will be conducted as needed and/or requested in a guest-host relationship with the government of the Republic of Vietnam. Reliance will be placed upon agreement and cooperation for the achievement of mutually advantageous objectives of the two governments.(17)

Civic Action in Vietnam:
the Picture at the End of June 1965

In June 1965, however, civic action in Vietnam at the battalion level remained in the advanced stages of a people-to-people program. The complete cycle of rural construction was being carried out only in Le My where unusually favorably circumstances had permitted the 2d Battalion, 3d Marines, to occupy the village and to cooperate with the district and village governing authorities. Elsewhere in June in the ICTZ, the Vietnamese government approved a massive expansion of the Marine Corps TAORs. As a direct result, the Marine Corps began an aggressive program of counterguerrilla operations in the midst of a moderately dense civilian population.(18) As the Marine

Corps began to contact the Viet Cong infrastructure through its operation at Le My and as a result of the counterguerrilla effort, it also began to coordinate its assistance to the rural population with the numerous U. S. government agencies in ICTZ. Simultaneously, various private U. S. assistance and relief organizations both in Vietnam and in the United States began to be synchronized with Marine Corps civic action. Finally, the first attack aircraft arrived at the Chu Lai airfield on 1 June 1965 and encouraged deeper moves against the main force of the Viet Cong, further expansion of the TAORs, and more sophisticated civic action.

III MAF had established an effective program of medical support for the rural population by June 1965. Permanent programs were set up in several fixed locations as contrasted with the numerous but irregular contacts made by individual Navy medical corpsmen operating with the daylight patrols. On 15 May 1965, at Le My, the 2d Battalion, 3d Marines, had begun to support a daily medical service. Corpsmen assisted local health workers there in providing medical treatment to the local people and helped to instruct the government medical trainees. The situation at Le My was ideal. The battalion was committed to the support of the Vietnamese rural construction cycle whereby the village would be returned to the control of local officials of the Republican government. Lieutenant Colonel Clement's battalion ensured the immediate physical security of the village and encouraged a self-help attitude amongst the officials and the citizens which would free the battalion as soon as possible from its support and security functions. The Marine Corps treated approximately 3,000 villagers each week at Le My; and, often the people required immediate evacuation to hospital facilities.(19)

Late in June and farther north in the Hue/Phu Bai TAOR, Lieutenant Colonel William W. Taylor's 3d Battalion, 4th Marines, established a weekly medical service in the villages of Thuy Phu, Thuy Long, and Thuy Than.(20) Civic action had developed slowly at Hue/Phu Bai because of the military and the demographic situations. There the 3d Battalion, 4th Marines was in an unusual tactical position. It was a single battalion defending an airfield and radio station isolated from the two large Marine Corps TAORs at Da Nang and Chu Lai. The defensive situation at Hue/Phu Bai was inherently more difficult than in the other Marine Corps areas; for example, no part of the TAOR at Hue/Phu Bai lay on the sea. The isolated and land-bound position of the 3d Battalion, 4th Marines was responsible for the battalion's emphasis on tactics and eventually the hard type of civic action, i.e., civic action which stressed security measures. The battalion's TAOR was also sparsely populated with most of the area hilly, covered with clear forest, and totally uninhabited.

During the first half of June 1965, the battalion had concentrated on visits by medical teams supported by powerful security detachments. The visits were important because of their immediate impact and their effectiveness in meeting a basic need of the peasantry. But the visits were irregular and had the nature of a warm, humanitarian gift rather than impersonal direct support for the local Vietnamese government. The battalion described its medical civic action as people-to-people medical assistance visits; the description illustrated the almost private nature of civic action as late as mid-June 1965.(21) But with the expansion of the TAOR on 15 June 1965 from 38 to 61 square miles, the civilian population increased from 8,000 to roughly 18,000 persons.(22) This latest expansion combined with the precise yet flexible instructions from HQ, III MAF helped to transform civic action into a regular program which would support the expanding counterguerrilla operations in the area and ultimately buttress Vietnamese rural construction.

In the Chu Lai area, two of the infantry battalions had established regular medical service by June 1965 while the 3d Battalion, 12th Marines, a more centrally located artillery battalion, provided a daily dispensary service in conjunction with Company B, 3d Medical Battalion. The Marine Corps TAOR around Chu Lai was expanded during June, and by the latter half of the month the Vietnamese government had given the Marine Corps the authority to conduct unilateral offensive operations within its limits. The Marine Corps began to place greater emphasis on patrolling and ambushing far out in the TAOR. The Marines developed a coherent system of defensive positions to stop enemy attacks which was known as the Forward Edge of the Battle Area (FEBA). The Marine Corps intended to protect the Chu Lai airfield by vigorous offensive action far from the field and anchored on the fixed positions of the FEBA. The rise in patrolling activity increased the necessity for a regular civic action program coordinated with the local Vietnamese officials. The 2d Battalion, 4th Marines began to operate a medical aid station at Ky Lien village every other day. Corpsmen provided medical treatment for 100-200 people during each visit of the medical team. The 3d Battalion, 3d Marines also provided medical assistance on a regular basis in its area of responsibility in the southern part of the Chu Lai TAOR in the District of Binh Son, Quang Ngai Province.(23) Between 25 May-15 June 1965, the TAOR was expanded from 55 to 101 square miles and the population increased from 23,000 to almost 56,000 civilians.(24) These changes in area and population initially interfered with the development and the continuity of Marine Corps civic action by focusing Marine Corps energies on the construction of new defensive positions as the FEBA expanded inland from the South China Sea.

The rough edges of Marine Corps civic action were still apparent in June 1965. First Lieutenant William F. B. Francis,

who had become Civil Affairs Officer of the 3d Marines on
15 April 1965, presented a picture of civic action which substantiated the preoccupation of the infantry battalions with
tactical missions and the association of civic action with
superficial people-to-people contact. Francis also made it
clear that the other U. S. military units in Vietnam in April
1965 had little to offer in the way of useful precedents. He
met a problem of obtaining basic supplies, e.g., medicine,
food, and clothing, for a civic action program and was forced
to obtain them largely as gifts. Clear, legitimate channels
of requisitioning and funding for civic action supplies took
time to establish. Coordination between the Marine Corps and
the various relief agencies including the U. S. Agency for
International Development and the Catholic Relief Society
(USAID and CRS) was slow in developing. Only a gratuitous
trickle of supplies for civic action was received until late
June 1965.(25)

Lieutenant Francis believed that the medical program in
1965 was the most important one in civic action. He emphasized
the necessity for continuity in medical civic action and
stated that "to treat /the people/ once and let them go did
absolutely nothing...They felt better for a little while, but
really it was ineffective unless continued treatment were
available."(26) Francis was critical of "pill patrols" amongst
the Special Forces, or small patrols accompanied by medical
personnel who would provide simple first aid. He emphasized
that the irregular approach represented by the small combat or
reconnaissance patrol "was almost a gimmick to win the favor
and attention of the people /in order/ to gain their confidence."(27) A medical facility operating at a fixed well-known
location in conjunction with a training program for Vietnamese
health workers was the best approach. Francis' basic opinion
of the civil affairs effort in Vietnam during the early summer
of 1965 was that the action "was enthusiastic but it was disorganized...just sort of groping and feeling with inadequate
supplies and personnel."(28)

Captain Lionel V. Silva, the Civil Affairs Officer of the
2d Battalion, 3d Marines painted a somewhat different picture.
His battalion engaged in an operation in the Le My area designed
to clear the Viet Cong from the village complex and to secure
the area for the GVN. The battalion commander and Captain Silva
soon learned that the temporary clearing of the Viet Cong was
relatively simple; for example, after one week of shooting
there were no more rifle-carrying Viet Cong within the village
complex. But the card-carrying Viet Cong of the infrastructue
remained and the population had not changed from its apathetic
attitude towards the government. Lieutenant Colonel Clement,
the battalion commander, thereupon decided to make his stand in
the village itself. Clement was fortunate in the location of
his TAOR. The larger Da Nang TAOR was expanded several times
during the pacification campaign, but the 2d Battalion, 3d Marines

Toys for little girls: two small waifs receive presents furnished through the U. S. Navy's Project Handclasp. 1stLt Brendan E. Cavanaugh makes the presentation in the village of Noa Thanh near Da Nang on 27 August 1965. (USMC A185025)

Candy was one of the basic commodities distributed during the early spontaneous days of civic action. In this picture taken on 10 September 1965 LtCol William F. Donahue, CO, 2nd Battalion, 9th Marines passes out candy to the children of Cam Ne (VI). This hamlet was located in the middle of a hard-core VC area only four miles southwest of Da Nang. (USMC A185697)

was able to secure its area of responsibility without a radical shift of its tactical positions. Continuity proved to be the keynote of success. The battalion established a dispensary which proved to be permanent because Vietnamese health workers were trained to staff it and were kept alive by Marine Corps rifles. Finally, and probably most important, local security forces were reestablished and were aggressively supported by the people.(29) Captain Silva, who was running the civic action program, showed insight into the problems of successful civic action when he said "it was obvious that we /would/ not always be in the Le My area. Even though we occupied it today, we knew that eventually our operations would necessitate our moving out."(30) Lieutenant Colonel Clement emphasized the same point. To him the essence of success was to create an administration supported by the people and capable of leading, treating, feeding, and protecting them by the time that the battalion was forced to leave.

But notwithstanding the individual success at Le My, the general picture of Marine Corps civic action was less a calculated effort at supporting local government and more an enthusiastic, irregular effort at medical assistance, support for local orphanages, efforts to improve communications, and various other activities. Lieutenant Francis painted the most accurate, general picture of civic action for the period March-May 1965. In June, however, HQ, III MAF provided central direction for the civic action effort in the form of concepts of civic action and the general picture began to change.

A Stormy Month and an Expanding Mission for III MAF

The transition from June to July 1965 in Vietnam was sharp and stormy for the Marine Corps. Early in the morning on 1 July 1965, Viet Cong forces attacked the southern end of the Da Nang Airbase between two fortified static posts. The attack was a raid conducted by small forces supported by 81mm mortars and probably one 57mm recoilless rifle. The Viet Cong in a stealthy, time-consuming operation cut their way through the wire obstacles at the southeast end of the runway. The cutting probably took more than 1-1/2 hours at the end of which time a coordinated attack took place. The mortars and the recoilless rifle fired for a period of four or five minutes. The fire was probably intended to inflict as much damage as possible while simultaneously suppressing resistance in the immediate area of the penetration so that Viet Cong with demolition charges could destroy the closest aircraft. The Viet Cong inflicted moderate damage during the attack and quickly retired after the demolitions thrust. Empty 81mm mortar cases found approximately 300 meters east of the runway testified to the boldness of the raid and the ineffectiveness of the boundaries of the Marine Corps TAOR. The Viet Cong had launched their raid from an area which was not part of the Marine Corps TAOR.(31)

HQ, III MAF reacted swiftly to the anomalies in the defensive situation to the east and south of the airbase. To ensure the defense of the airbase, the infantry battalion manning the defensive perimeter needed room to patrol, ambush, and maneuver several thousand meters forward of the perimeter. On 5 July 1965, CG, III MAF requested from CG, I Corps permission to enlarge the Marine Corps TAOR by moving eight kilometers into the densely populated rice growing region south of Da Nang to ensure adequate depth for the defense of the airbase. CG, I Corps sanctioned the expansion of the Marine Corps into the critical area south of Da Nang on 13 July 1965. Two days later, on 15 July 1965, CG, III MAF assumed responsibility for the area. The number of civilians under the control of the Marine Corps in the Da Nang **area** now totalled approximately 126,000 persons.(32) The raid on the Da Nang Airbase and its aftermath had deep repercussions in Marine Corps civic action. After 15 July 1965, III MAF came into direct competition with the Viet Cong for the loyalties and the support of the Vietnamese peasantry in a critical rice growing region immediately adjacent to a major city.

Nevertheless, Marine Corps civic action continued to have a people-to-people, or charitable ring to it. HQ, III MAF declared the objectives of Marine Corps civic action to be to gain support for the GVN and to win the confidence and cooperation of the Vietnamese civilians in the TAORS.(33) The Marine Corps, however, was not aware of the depth of Vietnamese efforts to win the struggle politically by means of rural construction. The Vietnamese government had placed heavy restrictions on the size of the Marine Corps TAORs and the missions to be performed inside of them because it doubted the ability of the Marine Corps to operate effectively in any of the densely populated areas of I Corps Tactical Zone. These restrictions and doubts were important reasons for the initial Marine Corps lack of concentration on the support of rural construction. For example, prior to 15 July 1965, the boundary of the Da Nang TAOR and the eastern defensive wire of the airbase coincided. The Marines were literally fenced in and physically cut off from the population to the east and south of the airbase. And they carried out little civic action on the uninhabited runway.

From March-July 1965, medical treatment was the most important civic action project of the Marine Corps. Teams of Marines, Navy medical corpsmen, and interpreters visited hamlets throughout the TAORs in a more advanced program than the original spontaneous efforts by combat patrols. In July alone approximately 29,000 civilians were treated for various minor ailments and a substantial number of people were evacuated for treatment of major afflictions. The number of treatments was impressive, but the real importance would be difficult to gauge. Medical teams made numerous treatments in unsecured areas where an appreciative but terrorized populace was simply unable to respond in any way beneficial to the Vietnamese cause. Probably the most important effort by July 1965 had been made at the permanent dispensary at Le My which operated on a daily schedule. The dispensary attracted a large number of Vietnamese peasants from miles around the village. The provision of regular service at central locations pointed the way to increased numbers of treatments for Vietnamese peasants and greater numbers of intelligence contacts for the Marine Corps. Probably most important though, regular treatment at fixed locations enabled the Marine Corps to train Vietnamese personnel to assist and eventually run the health centers which the people had come to appreciate. Short-term, high-impact medical visits at irregular times and in varying locations continued to be made effectively after July 1965.(34) But after that month a gradual shift began towards more direct support of the Vietnamese government in the form of regular service and the training of Vietnamese rural health workers.

Other civic action programs ranked below medical assistance in both general importance and immediate impact in the period March-July 1965. But some of the other programs were unusually simple and effective. A thing so humble in the United States as soap highlighted an important reality of disease and infection in Vietnam. Approximately 75 percent of the ailments treated by the medical teams were skin infections caused largely by the lack of knowledge of basic hygiene among mothers and persons who were responsible for the care of small children. The Vietnamese peasant quickly accepted soap as a beneficial addition to his existence. The transfer of soap between Marines and Vietnamese civilians became an important part of civic action from the lowest through the highest levels in III MAF. And the CG, Fleet Marine Force, Pacific (FMFPac) supported a campaign in the United States to collect soap for civic action.(35)

Units of III MAF distributed food and clothing in large quantities in South Vietnam. Sources of these basic commodities varied enormously and helped to direct Marine Corps attention to the problems of coordination among the numerous agencies and organizations competing to assist the rural population. Unused military rations, e.g., types C, B, and A, were passed on to especially needy Vietnamese individuals and families by Marine Corps units. In contrast with this spontaneous activity, III MAF received substantial quantities of wheat from the Catholic Relief Services, a powerful U. S. private relief organization which donated over 6,000 pounds of bulgur (a type of parched, crushed wheat) and delivered it to units of III MAF in Vietnam.(36) Clothing was a critical need for the Vietnamese people also, especially among the younger children. Parents and elders were often well-clothed because of their productive functions in a primitive rural society, but they neglected the satisfactory clothing of their younger children. The hot and humid climate of Vietnam was the reason for the physical neglect. The parents, who were certainly not apathetic towards their children, saw little reason for concern over clothing of the younger ones. But footwear, light clothes, and hats were necessary to counteract the hazards of infections from punctures, infestation by worms, and the effects of the sun. The July temperature variation was a hazard also; scantily-clad or naked children were apt to have common colds turn into serious upper respiratory infections and pneumonia. The Commanding Officer, 4th Marines was prompted by the needs of the peasants in the Chu Lai area to request his wife on the island of Oahu, Hawaii, to organize a drive for clothing and send the collected material to his regiment. Marine Corps wives on Oahu collected over 1,000 pounds of clothing for this humanitarian purpose, and the Marines in the Chu Lai TAOR distributed it to the most needy individuals and families that they were able to find through coordination with the local authorities.(37)

The Cooperative for American Relief Everywhere (CARE) and Project HANDCLASP were additional sources of civic action materials. CARE was a nonprofit, joint organization of 26 accredited American service agencies which had been formed in 1945 to help Americans overseas. Since that time, CARE has changed its emphasis to help human beings everywhere and has delivered almost one billion dollars worth of supplies overseas.(38) Project HANDCLASP was an official Navy program which had been formed in 1962 to promote mutual understanding between Americans and citizens of other lands. In June 1965, the Marine Corps units in Vietnam were brought into the program and shortly after that month began to receive HANDCLASP supplies for their civic action programs.(39)

On 5 July 1965, the first CARE supplies for III MAF arrived in Vietnam; the shipment was a humble beginning for a program with important possibilities for expansion by the Marine Corps. Two barrels of soap and two boxes of medical supplies comprised the first shipment. The directors of HANDCLASP delivered a substantial amount of supplies during July 1965 to Vietnam for distribution by III MAF. The relief and humanitarian nature of HANDCLASP as it applied to Vietnam was revealed in the shipping list of the first group of supplies. The first shipment, approximately 9,000 pounds of supplies, was comprised mainly of soap, buttons, thread, medicine, nutribio (a food supplement), and toys. Both CARE and HANDCLASP after humble beginnings, would become important sources of aid for Marine Corps civic action as III MAF expanded its TAORs and began to support Vietnamese local government and rural construction.

The provision of Marine Corps engineering and general construction assistance to Vietnamese in July 1965 highlighted the enforced limits of civic action during the first five months in Vietnam. Operational commitments minimized engineer work in support of civic action. The Marine Corps spent several months on the defensive in TAORs which were only gradually expanded. Construction of Main Lines of Resistance (later termed Forward

Edges of the Battle Area) took precedence over all building activity in the infantry battalions. And the engineer effort was split amongst airfield construction and engineer assistance for clearing new campsites, providing for area drainage, and constructing and repairing routes of communication within the expanding TAORs.(40) The continuous buildup of forces and the gradual movement inland and along the coast inhibited civic action construction projects.

The development of new life hamlets and the integration of refugees back into Vietnamese life were vital issues in the war and were affected by the initial defensive posture of the Marine Corps. III MAF units relocated civilian homes lying in fields of fire on the defensive perimeters surrounding the Da Nang Airbase and the Chu Lai Airfield. The movement of civilians under these circumstances was not the usual spontaneous and humanitarian thing on which the Marine Corps had concentrated. Coordination with the local governing officials proved difficult; this problem was reflected in the persistent return of displaced civilians to their cultivated plots. Additionally, the Marine Corps did not succeed in solving the problem of fair and timely payment of claims by the GVN.(41)

The First Five Months of Civic Action: Rising Emphasis on Support for Local Government

Nevertheless, the Marine Corps achieved substantial results in civic action during the first five months (March-July 1965) in Vietnam in the face of difficulties in emphasis, coordination, and adjustment. Command emphasis was primarily on the tactical integrity of the TAORs and secondarily on things like civic action. HQ, III MAF only gradually established coordination between its activities and those of HQ, I Corps Tactical Zone. The CG, I Corps remained suspicious of the intentions and the effectiveness of the Marine Corps and this fact interferred with coordination. But once General Walt had assured the tactical integrity of his TAORs, he proceeded to the long final step of determining what assistance the GVN required to win the rural struggle. The Marine Corps had required time to adjust to the movements of infantry battalions which were required to secure the expanding TAORs. III MAF also required time to develop and apply a sound theory of operations which took into account the necessity for security for the officials of the GVN who were executing the Republic's plan for rural construction. By the end of July, General Walt began to sense that civic action was the link between the Marine Corps tactical mission and Vietnamese rural construction.

Various factors by June and July 1965 pointed out the importance of purposeful civic action in support of the GVN. Continuous and regular medical support for the local population, either at fixed locations or at different locations on a fixed schedule, had proven to be extraordinarily effective. The increasing emphasis on regular service implied the integration of Marine Corps medical treatments with the struggling Vietnamese Rural Health Service. A vital link with the Vietnamese health program began to be forged by the training of rural health workers by corpsmen both in the Da Nang and Chu Lai areas.(42) The Commanding Officer, 4th Marines, Colonel Edward P. Dupras, Jr., set up a medical training program for Vietnamese health workers in his area on 23 June 1965. Colonel Dupras' effort was a pioneering one in the Chu Lai TAOR and revealed the trend towards civic action in direct support of the GVN.(43)

But coordination between HQ, III MAF and the U. S. Operations Mission in Vietnam, the civilian side of the American effort in the Republic was slow in developing. Medical Civic Action Program (MEDCAP) supplies were distributed by the U. S. Operations Mission to the U. S. agencies and forces in Vietnam. The Marine Corps received no MEDCAP supplies through regular channels in March-April 1965 and not until June were appreciable quantities received. For example, on 30 June 1965, the Marine Corps received 1,500 pounds (value $2,355.25) of medical supplies to be used during the month of July.(44) Coordination between the U. S. Operations Mission and III MAF was critical for both organizations. The mission had funds for medical supplies for support of rural construction but no operating personnel at the hamlet-village level.(45) The Marine Corps, on the other hand, had thousands of Marines and scores of doctors and corpsmen who were available as a concrete link between the U. S. government and the people of Vietnam at the hamlet level.

Throughout the first five months in Vietnam as Marine Corps support for Vietnamese rural construction began to coalesce, individual Marines launched spontaneous "programs" of their own which served as a powerful antidote to the Viet Cong propaganda which emphasized the brutality and ruthlessness of a foreign, professional, combat force. Sergeant John D. Moss of Marine Composite Reconnaissance Squadron (VMCJ) 1 bought a small horse in mid-June 1965 near the Da Nang Airbase.(46) Sergeant Moss then went into the free pony ride business and brought brief happiness and lasting memories into the lives of many innocents. Less well known was the anonymous Marine who impressed Mr. Nguyen Dinh Nam, Village Chief of Hoa Than (directly west of Da Nang). After observing Marine Corps operations for three months, Mr. Nam wrote a letter expressing the emotions of the people in Northwest Hoa Vang towards the Marine Corps. Both he and the rural population were especially impressed by the spontaneous humanity of the combat Marines. Mr. Nam noted the following:

Medical evacuation: a Vietnamese farmer waits for helicopter evacuation on 5 May 1965 northwest of Da Nang. Sgt Dubry, Company G, 2nd Battalion, 3rd Marines, is in immediate command of the move. Evacuation of seriously sick or injured civilians was an important part of the Medical Civic Action Program. (USMC A184126)

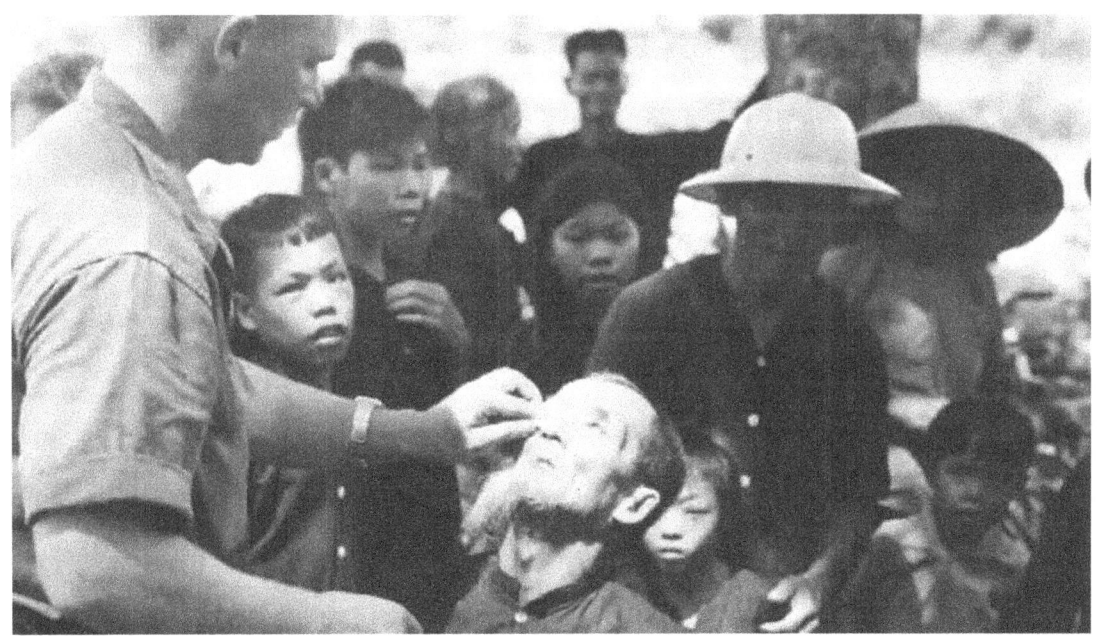

Eye ailments: infections of the eyes were notoriously common in Vietnam and were the result largely of missing emphasis on the use of soap and water. In this scene HM-2 M.E. Prigmore assists an old grey-beard while a probable father and small daughter wait their turn. Note the curious but apprehensive spectator at lower right. (USMC A184659)

> They /the Marines/ have all the favorable attitudes towards the people of this area. For example, it was noted that one officer of the rank of Major while walking saw a child whose foot was bleeding. He stopped and was happy to dress the boy's foot.(47)

Various Marine Corps combat and supporting organizations carried out humanitarian civic action which was imaginative and resourceful. On Monday 19 July 1965, Company D, 1st Battalion, 3d Marines purchased a young water buffalo for 4,000 piasters ("tourist" rate of exchange approximately 75 piasters to one dollar) at Hoa Thinh, a village complex located a few miles southwest of the Da Nang Airbase. The company planned to raise the buffalo and then give it to an especially needy family.(48) Closer to the center of the TAOR, the Force Logistics Support Group (FLSG) after its formation in the Da Nang area, began to support local charitable organizations. Members of the FLSG discovered that in the Sacred Heart Orphanage, a struggling religious charity, flour for bread was being provided in moderate quantities from Vietnamese government sources. But the Catholic sisters operating the charity seemed less pleased than they should have been with the generosity of the government. The FLSG soon found the answer to the paradox. The orphanage had no facilities for baking bread and the sisters had to deal with a city bakery which took half of the flour as the charge for preparing the remainder as bread. The HQ, FLSG, put available Marine Corps ovens to work in support of the handful of sisters and their brood of helpless and unwanted youngsters. One thousand pounds of bread were soon baked for the cause of the Sacred Heart.

The efforts of Marine Corps civic action were difficult to measure in terms of advances in the struggle against the Viet Cong. HQ, III MAF began to collect statistics on the number of medical treatments rendered, pounds of food and clothing distributed, etc.. But the correlation between medical treatments and the erosion of the Viet Cong political and military effort was too complex for definition. For example, how many civic action medical treatments advanced the Republican cause a certain percent towards final victory in the war? Questions of this sort were possible to broach; however, they were impossible to answer. Probably the most effective correlation between civic action and the struggle against the Viet Cong was information received from the peasants about the movements, activities, and plans of the rural communists. But the receipt of information of intelligence value was more dependent on calculated and effective security than warm, spontaneous, and humanitarian civic action. Nevertheless, there was a close relationship between security and civic action. Whenever Marine Corps civic action took place, Marine Corps rifles provided security, unwittingly at first in many cases but eventually on purpose. And in spite of the lack of a precise mathematical correlation between medical treatments for Vietnamese civilians and progress against the Viet Cong, there was an indisputable increase in hard information about the enemy.(49)

Why was this information important? The Viet Cong existed only with the silence of the rural population. Viet Cong movement and functioning was impossible in the event of general disclosure by the peasantry. Lawrence of Arabia, two generations ago spelled out the reality of a successful guerrilla movement in a brief thought--a civilian population unwilling to disclose the presence and movements of the guerrilla functionaries. Lawrence's thought was a function of his experience in the sparsely populated Northwestern Arabian Peninsula. In the densely populated areas around Da Nang, guerrillas were even less able to move without the knowledge of the peasantry. Viet Cong success depended on muting the local people and this was done by a combination of physical terror and hope for a better future life. The emphasis was on terror, however, and any successful counteraction by the Marine Corps and the Vietnamese government would have to take the form of either more effective terror or decisive security against the Viet Cong atrocities.(50) The Viet Cong promise of a brighter future would have to be undercut by an effective program of rural construction on the part of the Republic and civic action by the Marine Corps.

The success of Marine Corps civic action could be measured by the receipt of intelligence information from the peasantry. And because the peasants provided information only with adequate security, the providing of intelligence information became one of the best indicators of progress in the war. Reliable information began to increase by mid-June 1965, and by July, peasants were providing information in a large number of exchanges. For example, on 10 July 1965, the peasants at Le My reported that route 545 (see Map Number One) was mined just north of Hill 282. Two days later, the 1st Battalion, 3d Marines reported that civilians from Thinh Tay had exposed the presence of a Viet Cong company located approximately 1,200 meters southwest of the district headquarters at Hieu Duc in notorious "Happy Valley" (see Map Number One). Marine Corps infantry battalions which had won the confidence of the people by careful attention to their feelings and needs were sometimes rewarded with remarkably precise and valuable information. On 24 July 1965, a woman living in Kinh Than reported that two days earlier, 100 Viet Cong carrying small arms including one automatic rifle and each carrying one grenade passed by her home. She also noted that the Viet Cong were wearing black uniforms and carrying rice in long cloth rolls.(51)

Civilians like the woman of Kinh Thanh repaid heavy investments in civic action. The Viet Cong insurgency was simply not possible with a population of similar people. Civic action aimed to create peasants who recognized the Marine Corps as a benevolent protector and who were willing to work hand in hand with the Republican government for the advancement of the rural areas. And the concept began to emerge that Marine Corps combat operations against the main and guerrilla forces of the Viet Cong were not solely for the purpose of inflicting casualties. The higher Marine Corps leadership began to visualize the combat operations as the screen behind which Vietnamese rural construction could progress and "the other war" could finally be won.

Chapter V

A Turning Point
August 1965

August 1965 ushered in a fresh realization of the importance of civic action. HQ, III MAF and the infantry battalions had learned that successful engagements against main force enemy units and interference with the movements of guerrillas were of little importance if the GVN was unable to fill the resulting political and military vacuum. In the area to the south of the Da Nang air base, the GVN was unable either to execute an effective program of rural construction or to reconstruct Republican government, and the 9th Marines was obliged to carry out operations behind its frontline positions because of the presence of a Viet Cong dominated peasantry in Cam Ne village.(1) These operations called attention to the need for much greater coordination between HQ, III MAF and the Vietnamese government in the northern region. The Vietnamese government was meeting heavy weather south of Da Nang and the Marine Corps had to trim its combat sails in order to assist Vietnamese rural construction behind the Marine Corps FEBA. On 7 August 1965, General Walt assumed operational control of the I Corps Advisory Group, a task which carried with it the necessity for increased knowledge of Vietnamese plans and capabilities.(2)

The general situation in August demanded more effective coordination between the commanders, politicians, and functionaries who disposed of the resources for combatting the Viet Cong. HQ, III MAF had coordinated extensively with the Vietnamese authorities prior to August 1965, but the most effective aims for Marine Corps civic action had not yet been determined. At the battalion level, civic action continued to have the spirit of an enthusiastic people-to-people effort rather than a program synchronized towards a single decisive goal.(3) For example, the diffuse idea of winning the people was simply not enough to direct a useful program of civic action. The GVN, the U. S. Operations Mission, and the Marine Corps were winning the people; but, the Vietnamese Government was unable to secure areas cleared by the Marine Corps and ARVN combat units. General Walt needed a firmer target for civic action. He had to know two things: first, the Republic's rural construction plans, and second, the resources available in ICTZ to support those plans. To discover those things he needed a better system of coordination between himself and the authorities of the Vietnamese state.

The Formation of the I Corps Joint Coordinating Council: late August 1965

But the complexities of fighting in a foreign, sovereign state presented problems. Neither the United States nor South Vietnam would accept a single military commander and staff. Yet the Republican Government required the efficient use of all of the resources available for the struggle if it were ever to reestablish control over its Northern Region. The situation called for great tact; both the United States and Vietnamese authorities required a coordinating body to ensure the use of available resources in support of an effective plan for the survival of the Vietnamese government. "Pursuant to the August 25, 1965, conversation between General L. W Walt...and Mr. Marcus J. Gordon, Regional Director USOM /United States Operations Mission/, I Corps, the first meeting of a permanent regional working group was convened on August 30, 1965."(4) The Civil Affairs Officer of III MAF had suggested on 29 August 1965 that the coordinating council which had been created several days earlier by the meeting between Walt and Gordon be called the I Corps Joint Coordinating Council (I Corps JCC). The term, council, had no connotation in the Republic of Vietnam which precluded its use. The term, joint, was used because General Walt and Mr. Gordon intended that the Vietnamese as well as the Americans be represented.

The establishment of the I Corps JCC was a milestone in the development of Marine Corps civic action in Vietnam. The mission of the council spelled out the importance of Vietnamese rural construction and was intended to ensure maximum support for it. The I Corps JCC was to become familiar with the GVN's rural construction program in the ICTZ. Having become familiar with the plan, the I Corps JCC was to determine the requirements for cooperation and support between agencies and to recommend methods or procedures to meet the requirements.(5)

General Walt, who had been designated as Senior U. S. Military Advisor to the CG, I Corps, earlier in August 1965, intended that the I Corps JCC focus Marine Corps civic action on a concrete central mission, essentially that of supporting Vietnamese rural construction. General Walt also intended that all of the U. S. agencies and private organizations operating in ICTZ be synchronized in support of rural construction by a regional-level coordinating body. The Senior (Vietnamese) Government Delegate in the First Region was immediately aware of the importance of the council. General Thi met with General Walt on 28 September 1965 and agreed to the formation and purposes of the I Corps JCC and appointed Lieutenant Colonel Cach, I Corps Rural Construction Officer, as the government liaison officer to the council.

The I Corps JCC rapidly became the coordinating hub for the civil activities of most of the U. S. governmental agencies in the Northern Region of Vietnam. In addition to the representatives of the Vietnamese government and HQ, III MAF, membership on the council included members of the following U. S. military, naval, and civilian agencies:

      a. I Corps Advisory Group, MACV.
      b. MACV Combined Studies Division.
      c. Naval Support Activity, Da Nang.
      d. U. S. Embassy, Political Advisor on Staff, III MAF.
      e. U. S. Agency for International Development, 1st Region.
      f. Joint U. S. Public Affairs Office, 1st Region.

The formation of the council under the auspices of the CG, III MAF focused Marine Corps attention on the importance of the other war in Vietnam and was a powerful boost for organized civic action.(6) But rural construction was a complex thing and the members of the council had to establish several working committees to assist them in accomplishing their mission. The committees, within their assigned fields, monitored the development of U. S. and Vietnamese plans for future action and determined the capabilities of the U. S. and Vietnamese military organizations and civilian agencies to support the plans. The committees which were formed by the I Corps JCC read like a list of civic action programs. The following were in operation by January 1966:(7)

      a. Public Health   d. Commodities Distribution
      b. Education   e. Psychological Warfare
      c. Roads   f. Port of Da Nang

General Walt realized, and his feelings were shared by the Commanding General, Fleet Marine Force, Pacific, Lieutenant General Victor H. Krulak, that the central issue of the struggle was the reinstitution of Republican political control over the rural areas. But Walt knew that the lasting control, which had eluded the Marine Corps in its embryonic efforts against the Viet Cong from March-August 1965, would result only from an indigenous political effort. In turn, Marine Corps civic action could provide vital support for the government's effort only if HQ, III MAF, knew the government's plans, both political and military. In the Marine Corps scheme of things, civic action linked Vietnamese rural construction with the combat operations of the Marine air-ground team. To underscore the importance of the I Corps JCC, General Walt designated Brigadier Generals Keith B. McCutcheon and Melvin D. Henderson to sit on the council replacing the former colonel "to ensure that the III MAF /was/ giving the council the best possible support in its program of assisting the government of Vietnam in the execution of its rural construction program in the ICTZ."(8) The two generals began to represent the Marine Corps on 15 November 1965.

Golden Fleece

At the highest level the month of August 1965 was a milestone in the synchronization of Marine Corps civic action with Vietnamese rural construction. But farther down the chain of command, Marines developed several projects which proved to be of lasting importance. Lieutenant Colonel Verle E. Ludwig, Commanding Officer, 1st Battalion, 9th Marines, controlled a sector which included four villages and numerous hamlets. Ludwig took a deep interest in the village chiefs and made effective efforts to support their authority and to provide for the real needs of their people. As the price for Marine Corps efforts, Ludwig sought information of intelligence value about the Viet Cong. The battalion formed a joint "Area Security Council" and conducted a vigorous and effective counter-guerrilla campaign which totally changed the balance of power in its TAOR. The peasants, like those at Le My, soon were convinced that the battalion was able to protect them from the Viet Cong. After a particularly aggressive Marine Corps sweep through the battalion TAOR on 29 August 1965, Huynh Ba Trinh, Village Chief of Hoa Hai, "said that the villagers were impressed by the U. S. Marines and wanted to know if /they/ would help them protect their rice crop from the Viet Cong tax."(9) The chain of events was ideal. The peasants needed assistance and had requested it through their government leader. The Marine Corps was presented with a golden opportunity to support a representative of the local government and to fulfill a basic need of a large number of people. Lieutenant Colonel Ludwig's efforts at coordination, and demonstrations of Marine Corps superiority over the Viet Cong, were fused with the basic needs of a terrorized and partly starved population. Lieutenant Colonel Ludwig accepted the invitation to protect the rice crop and Operation GOLDEN FLEECE was born.

HQ, III MAF seized the opportunity offered in the area of the 1st Battalion, 9th Marines, and by mid-September 1965, GOLDEN FLEECE operations were absorbing the energies of a full Marine regiment and were taking place both in the Da Nang and Chu Lai areas. The Marine Corps took the initiative from the Viet Cong in the critical field of food supply. Marine Corps infantry battalions forced the Viet Cong to fight for rice which had been uncontested for the last two years of Republican weakness.

A major strength of the Viet Cong had been its lack of dependence on fixed supporting installations. Conversely, in order to maintain the image and the reality of political control, the Republican government had to protect fixed installations and areas. The Viet Cong could be likened to bank robbers in a city who had the practical advantages of surprise in point and place of robbery, and the psychological advantages of being daring, resourceful individuals aligned against the police forces of an existing regime. The government and Viet Cong roles were not completely reversed during the GOLDEN FLEECE operations, but only one rice bank could be robbed during the harvest of autumn 1965. Finally, the Robin Hood diguise of the Viet Cong was wearing thin by 1965. The Vietnamese peasantry, in spite of the heady Viet Cong promises for the future and the enforcement of terror in the present, had requested assistance from the Marine Corps. The request of the people for protection against the Viet Cong was the most important fact about GOLDEN FLEECE.

The GOLDEN FLEECE operations in autumn 1965 effectively harassed the Viet Cong. The latter had been so successful during 1963-1964 that they controlled large areas of the rich rice lands in the ICTZ, i.e., the bank robbers had done so well that they owned and occupied the northern rice bank by 1965. But vested interests were anathema to guerrilla movements. The strength of the Viet Cong lay in the ability to choose the weakest of a multitude of opposing installations and launch well-planned attacks against them in overwhelming strength.(10) Operation GOLDEN FLEECE forced the Viet Cong either to give up an installation on which they had come to depend after two years of exploitation, or fight on Marine Corps terms. Discretion was the better part of Viet Cong valor. The Viet Cong lost probably 90 percent of the unrefined rice that they could reasonably have expected to collect based on their "tax receipts" during the preceding harvest.(11)

The Importance of Local Security: Development of the Combined Action Company Concept

The Marine Corps developed another scheme in August 1965 which provided hard security for the peasants and supported rural construction. Security for the Republic's hamlet dwellers was the beginning and the end of rural construction, and already by August, the Marine Corps was providing it against main force Viet Cong units. For example, on 18 August 1965, the 7th Marines launched Operation STARLITE (18-21 August) against a main force regiment and obliterated it. Reliable body count set the Viet Cong dead at 699 and intelligence follow-up revealed probable losses of 1,400 dead including a general officer.(12) And equally as important as success in large unit operations, III MAF launched a program of saturation patrolling and ambushing during the hours of both daylight and darkness. Marines moved freely in "Viet Cong country" 24 hours a day and this professional effort became the shield behind which the Vietnamese government could reestablish control over the countryside. For any lasting effort, however, the government and not the Marine Corps would have to protect the rural population; but, government was something which had its foundation in the people. The government officials and the people ultimately had to protect themselves; and, the best

Golden Fleece: the operations which were called Golden Fleece began in August 1965 in the Da Nang TAOR and rapidly spread to other Marine areas. In this picture taken in September, Marine rifles protect peasants carrying rice to amphibious tracked vehicles (LVTP-5) for transport to a secure area. Golden Fleece was a response to local calls for aid. (MCA185781)

Soap and water: lack of personal hygiene was responsible for the high incidence of skin disease among children and adults in Vietnam. In this scene Marines wash a little boy as a lesson for the mothers of Thuy Tan village west of Hue/Phu Bai in Sep 65. LtCol Khoa, Province Chief of Thua Thien, evidently approves of this joint operation. (USMC A185541)

form of self-help for the people was participation in the security effort against the Viet Cong terror.

The Vietnamese people helped to protect themselves locally by forming Popular Force platoons which were used at the hamlet and village level.(13) Some of the better trained and motivated platoons produced remarkable results. But in general, the equipment and training of the platoons and their unimaginative use in static defensive positions made them a slender reed in the fight against the Viet Cong. The latter were able to concentrate themselves at leisure against the fixed posts of the Popular Forces and by launching attacks with a predetermined crushing superiority in numbers and firepower were able to overwhelm them with ominous regularity.

During August 1965, however, in the Hue/Phu Bai area, the Marine Corps with the cooperation of several village chiefs formed a Joint Action Company to meet the problem of local security. Both the Marines and Vietnamese knew the limitations of the Popular Forces but wanted to place local security on Vietnamese shoulders. Several village chiefs agreed to allow four Popular Force platoons to work directly with four Marine rifle squads. The resultant force was called a Joint Action Company and was commanded by a Marine Corps officer who used the Marines to train the Popular Forces in small unit tactics, marksmanship, etc., and to serve as the nucleus for patrols and ambushes throughout the village area assigned to each platoon. The joint platoons would also conduct vigorous civic action programs in support of the local governing officials. The program would emphasize self-help by the peasants in the civic action projects while security would be provided by the joint platoons.(14)

By 14 August 1965 the CG, 1st Vietnamese Army Division, had assigned six Popular Force platoons in the Hue/Phu Bai area to the operational control of the CO, 3d Battalion, 4th Marines. The latter ensured the coordination of operations within the battalion TAOR by providing communications between the Joint Action Company and the battalion's combat operations center. Additionally, a Marine Corps officer with a knowledge of the Vietnamese language commanded the company and a Vietnamese officer acted as executive officer facilitating cooperation in both directions--Vietnamese and Marine Corps. The Joint Action Company immediately freed one Marine Corps rifle company from security duty within the perimeter. The concept promised to free the attached Marine rifle squads as soon as the Popular Forces had received the training and gained the confidence to defeat the Viet Cong alone.

The integration of Marines into Popular Force platoons was successful from the beginning. In an "exclusive interview" with a reporter of the Los Angeles Times, General Walt revealed on 21 September 1965, that the concept was being tested and emphasized that the integration did not involve first line Vietnamese soldiers.(15) General Walt cautiously revealed the integration because of the implications of foreign military control over Vietnamese forces. Walt's caution was also justified in order to reduce the impact of any unforeseen setback in the program. By the end of September, though, it was evident that the program was developing successfully and General Walt publically announced a new and successful program in civic action.

The ultimate importance of the integration program or Combined Action Companies--the present term for the former Joint Action Companies--was the support provided for Vietnamese revolutionary development. Captain Francis J. West, Jr., writing at first hand about the Combined Action Companies, had the following to say concerning their broader implications:

> Properly used and supervised, the CAC can become a catalyst for development at the village level. Where there are Revolutionary Development Teams it can aid and support them. Where there are no Revolutionary Development Teams it can work to help the Popular Forces and hamlet chiefs and elders bring about change and progress. CAC is an interim program designed to assist the Vietnamese. It is not designed to displace the village leadership or replace the Revolutionary Development Program. Quite the contrary...village chiefs and Revolutionary Development Team Leaders have been quick to use the CAC units in their support.(16)

Support for Civic Action from the United States: the Reserve Civic Action Fund

While the development of civic action was accelerating in August 1965 with the appearance of the GOLDEN FLEECE and the CAC concepts, the Marine Corps began a notable program of support for civic action on a nation-wide scale in the United States. Captain Rodgers T. Smith, who was stationed at HQ, U. S. Marine Corps, Division of Reserve, and several other officers knew that tools, food, medicine, and other necessities were in short supply for Vietnamese civilians within the Marine TAORs despite government and private assistance efforts. Yet thousands of Marines were in close, daily contact with Vietnamese civilians at the hamlet level and were available to distribute additional supplies. At the same time thousands of Marine Corps reservists were anxious to assist their regular comrades by contributions of their own. An effective system would have been to purchase supplies in the United States and ship them overseas to III MAF which had the Marines and the machines to distribute them. But shipping space was at a premium as a result of the buildup in Vietnam, and the purchase of commodities directly by Marines was prohibited by Marine Corps policy.(17)

Claims against the Marine Corps: damage to crops and homes and injuries to civilians were the inevitable result of a war amongst the people. In this picture taken south of Da Nang on 13 Aug 65 the CG, III MAF himself presents a new motor-bike to a claimant. The civilian (right) was struck by a Marine truck which destroyed his former bike. (USMC A184977)

Clothes for old men: the warm scarf was contributed from the United States to Marines of III MAF who in turn arranged for its presentation to a citizen of Vietnam through officials of the government. In this scene an ARVN soldier contributes the scarf in June 1965 to a needy farmer under pleasant and effective circumstances. Note the waif lower right. (USMC A184687)

With these problems in mind, Major Glenn B. Stevens and Captain Smith visited the Washington office of CARE on 24 August 1965 and discussed ways that the Marine Corps Reserve and CARE could alleviate the suffering of human beings in Vietnam and further the cause of Marine Corps civic action.(18) The Marine Corps officers and the Director of the Washington CARE Office, Mrs. Ruth M. Hamilton, rapidly worked out a mutually agreeable plan. Marines would collect no monies; instead, each Marine in the reserve would contribute directly to CARE offices throughout the United States in envelopes marked specifically for the "Marine Corps Reserve Civic Action for Vietnam." CARE would then purchase the needed supplies and deliver them to the III MAF. To avoid the bottleneck in shipping space from the United States and to assist the Vietnamese economy, CARE would purchase as much of the supplies as possible within Vietnam itself. The Commandant of the Marine Corps launched the program officially on 13 September 1965 and emphasized that the conduct of a joint Marine Corps Reserve/CARE Program was a task short of mobilization for which the Reserve was singularly well-qualified.(19) The Reserve did not disappoint the Commandant; by 3 January 1966 it had contributed over $100,000 and simultaneously had carried out a bit of civic action in the United States--the annual Toys for Tots Program.(20)

Chapter VI

Accelerating the Pace of Civic Action
The Challenge of Support of Rural Construction
(September-December 1965)

For the Marines in Vietnam, the month of September 1965 was one of expanding civic action programs and increasing emphasis on patrolling and ambushing. Patrols and ambushes began to mesh more closely with civic action and rural construction. Both of the latter were possible only with the security for the operators of the civic action medical teams, Vietnamese People's Action Teams, etc. Operations like STARLITE and PIRANHA (7-10 September 1965) against main force Viet Cong units reduced the chances of overt action against the air facilities in the Marine Corps TAORs.(1) But these operations took place in peripheral population areas and had no direct effect on the people. The Viet Cong defeats, however, affected the enemy's tactics in all of the Marine Corps TAORs. The defeats convinced the Viet Cong that the best way to maintain their influence was to intensify guerrilla warfare aimed at positive control over an expanding number of hamlets. Expensive large scale victories or more probable defeats at the hands of a flexibly maneuvered Marine Corps with superior firepower were to be avoided. By early October 1965, the joint Marine Corps and ARVN effort to win in the northern region had forced the Viet Cong into the tactics of small unit guerrilla warfare. But the deeply intrenched Viet Cong infrastructure and associated guerrilla bands were an enemy which in turn required changes in tactics on the part of the Marine Corps.(2)

To defeat the Viet Cong at the enduring grass roots level, a dramatic increase in Marine Corps civic and small unit counter-guerrilla action took place between October-December 1965. Patrols and ambushes in October totalled 5,327 separate actions; by December the total was 7,206. Marine Corps personnel strength remained almost stationary during the period(3) thus supporting the view that III MAF had partly shifted its emphasis to small unit action in support of civic action and rural construction. Within the civic action program proper, medical treatment was probably the best indicator of trends towards either the expansion or contraction of the program. Medical treatment was largely the result of command emphasis within III MAF and was not so dependent on outside sources of transportation and similar factors, as for example the receipt and distribution of food and clothing. III MAF, working through a practically stable number of Marines, raised the number of Vietnamese civilians treated medically from approximately 43,000 in October 1965 to almost 61,000 in December 1965.(4)

After August 1965, Marine Corps civic action began to pass out of the stage of people-to-people activity and into the stage of linking Marine Corps civic action with Vietnamese rural construction. The I Corps Joint Coordinating Council, with its plainly announced purpose of supporting Vietnamese political activity in the countryside, forced the synchronization of civic action with Vietnamese plans for political, social, and economic change. Changes in Marine Corps organization reflected the increased emphasis on civic action. Until October 1965, many battalion, regimental, and divisional civil affairs billets had been additional duty assignments. For example, the Civil Affairs Officer of the 2d Battalion, 3d Marines during the Le My pacification program had been primarily the Intelligence Officer of the battalion. Late in October 1965, the Civil Affairs Section of the special staff at HQ, III MAF was changed to a fifth general staff section. The Civil Affairs Officer became the G-5 of III MAF and plans were made to transfer the Psychological Warfare Section from the G-3 Section to the G-5. The G-5 officer became responsible for civic action and psychological warfare and had as primary assistants a Civic Action Officer and a Psychological Warfare Officer.(5)

The formation of a G-5 Section at HQ, III MAF led to the formation of similar general staff sections within many of the headquarters elements of the 3d Marine Division and the 1st Marine Air Wing. However, all of the appropriate subordinate units of III MAF were not able to form G- or S-5 sections. Regiments and battalions were generally involved monthly in operations against the main force of the Viet Cong and these combat efforts in addition to the counter-guerrilla operations necessitated the use of most officers in combat billets. Most commanders were aware of the importance of civic action, especially when they began to realize that their combat efforts were reduced in value by ineffective Vietnamese rural construction and poorly coordinated Marine Corps civic action. But the large unit combat missions and the burgeoning counter-guerrilla actions took most of the energies of the battalions and practically all of the available personnel. Nevertheless, the regiments and air groups soon had either full-time Civil Affairs Officers or S-5 Officers and the battalions and squadrons attempted to follow suit. As early as October 1965 the 3d Battalion, 9th Marines established an S-5 Section which was responsible for the civic action and the psychological warfare effort of the battalion. HQ, III MAF remained flexible in the matter of organization and promulgated no directives which enforced a standard organization for civic action throughout III MAF.

The formation of the I Corps Joint Coordinating Council and the establishment of G-5 and S-5 sections began the decisive coordination of civic action with rural construction and gave III MAF the interal organization to ensure the support of the latter. The Viet Cong ran afoul of the increasingly effective Marine Corps civic action in October 1965 during the dramatic attack against the Marble Mountain air facility near Da Nang. The action was a typical well-planned but rigidly executed Viet Cong raid. Numerous enemy units were involved in the action. A main force battalion moved out of Happy Valley ten miles southwest of the Da Nang Airbase with the apparent intention of attacking the base from the west and creating a diversion for the demolitions experts at Marble Mountain.(6) On the same night, 27/28 October 1965, Company I, 3d Battalion, 9th Marines acting on information gleaned through civic action rapport with the local civilians set up an ambush approximately 1,100 meters south of Bo Mung (see Map Number One) on a trail known to the Marines as Henderson Road. The reinforced squad comprising the patrol waited only 30 minutes before elements of a heavily armed force of approximately company strength heading east blundered into the ambush. Captain Thomas F. McGowan, Executive Officer of the company, who debriefed the patrol leader, was not certain that the ambush had struck the advanced elements of a company. But he noted that the ambush contacted a large group, probably 70-100 men. Fifteen Viet Cong were killed in the action and the large number of dead supported a view that the group had a mission which involved a determined thrust past any resistance which it might encounter in the vicinity of Bo Mung.(7)

By October 1965, civic action had become an efficient program in most of the Marine Corps battalions and squadrons. The stabilization of the TAORs and the presence of a large civilian population had placed the Marine Corps in close contact with the peasants. The 3d Battalion, 9th Marines had checked a Viet Cong thrust through its area on 27 October 1965 largely as a result of information received from civilians who had come to respect Marine Corps humanity more than they feared Viet Cong terror. The battalion had a civic action program in October which was transitional between the people-to-people idea and the concept of deliberate support for Vietnamese rural construction. Its program was representative of Marine Corps civic action towards the end of 1965.

HQ, 3d Battalion, 9th Marines connected psychological warfare with civic action within an S-5 Section and in October employed the Vietnamese I Corps Psychological Warfare Battalion Audio Team on seven different occasions amongst its "frontline companies." The battalion originated several leaflets as reactions to specific incidents, e.g., Vietnamese children wounded by Viet Cong mortars, civilian casualties from Marine Corps fire, movement of the battalion dispensary, etc.. The psychological warfare program was designed to react to predictable incidents, to prepare the local population for initial contacts with the Marine Corps, and to condition the civilians of any operational area towards responses favorable to the battalion. Four helicopter broadcasts were made in October 1965

warning the people to take cover when the Viet Cong were in
their area, and a total of 125,000 pieces of propaganda
material were dropped in five additional helicopter missions.(8)

The HQ, 3d Battalion, 9th Marines ensured effective liaison
with the Vietnamese government and representatives of the U. S.
Operations Mission in its TAOR. The battalion made special
efforts at the District/Sub Sector level to coordinate support
for the Nine-Village Hoa Vang Pacification Plan and to avoid
duplication of effort. The medical program continued to be
the most important for civic action. Battalion medical personnel treated 1,842 Vietnamese civilians; approximately 80 percent
of the people treated were children under 18 years of age. The
battalion clearly delineated its short-range projects which
were similar to those in most battalion-level units. The
projects included the following:(9)

    a. Medical assistance including evacuation
    b. Soap distribution
    c. Food distribution
    d. Market Areas
    e. Damage claims
    f. Civic action orientation for Marines
    g. Civilian collection points during tactical operations

The 3d Battalion, 9th Marines was not a completely representative battalion, however, and its programs were unusual in
their emphasis on psychological warfare and their opportunity
for support of the Republic's rural construction in the nine
villages south of the Cau Do River in Hoa Vang district.(10)
The battalion cleared that area in cooperation with other
Marine Corps units and the Vietnamese Army. Following the
clearing action, the Chief of Quang Nam province sent survey
teams into the area to take a census, to determine the needs
of the villagers, to identify the Viet Cong infrastructure,
and to prepare plans for rural construction. Training of
Vietnamese personnel to carry out the tasks of rural construction went on concurrently, and by the end of October 1965,
People's Action Teams were ready to bring a new life to Hoa Vang
with the critical support of one Regional Force battalion. In
this area III MAF rubbed shoulders with a major Vietnamese
rural construction project for the first time. But with the
orientation of the Marine Corps forward in the TAOR, the
responsibility for the security of the rural construction project fell on the shoulders of the Regional and Popular Forces
whose training and equipment were not fully effective.(11)

Civic Action in November 1965:
First Contact with a Major Rural Construction Project

On 1 November 1965 the intensive rural construction effort
began in Hoa Vang district. The 59th Regional Force Battalion

was committed alongside of a Rural Construction organization of 350 trained Rural Construction personnel who received salaries from the Vietnamese government. The 3d Battalion, 9th Marines coordinated closely with the Regional and Popular Forces and the rural construction workers and provided nighttime security for the People's Action Teams within the tactical areas of Companies I and L. The Vietnamese conducted patrols, initiated a census, and began political and psychological warfare operations in the hamlets. As November 1965 drew to a close, the census had been completed, schools were reopening, and local government was budding into life. But security for the rural construction effort depended on local Popular Forces and these had not been brought under the control of the Marine Corps for training and tactical direction. The Popular Forces were ignored by the ARVN, unpaid by the GVN, poorly armed, and defensively oriented. Nevertheless, the Popular Forces were the main target of Viet Cong attacks. And without them, the well-trained rural construction cadre were forced to defend themselves rather than provide direction for a new life in the nine villages.(12)

The campaign made its greatest progress in Hoa Thai village where III MAF forces provided security for the young paramilitary and political shock troops. But within the village complex the two hamlets of Cam Ne and Yen Ne proved especially difficult to dominate and the rural construction workers were unable to finish the securing stages of rural construction before the defending Marine battalion moved its security forces outward towards the FEBA. On 21 December 1965, elements of the 59th Regional Forces Battalion, which had taken over the security of the hamlets, were attacked by a force of 50-60 Viet Cong. The peasants of Cam Ne and Yen Ne had probably sheltered the Viet Cong for two days prior to the attack. Rural construction came to a halt; the rural construction workers were withdrawn from the hamlets and a reinforced rifle company of the 3d Battalion, 3d Marines began a methodical sweep of the area. Rural construction cadre were not reintroduced until January 1966.(13)

The I Corps JCC, assured of the full support of Generals Walt and Thi, assisted in the coordination of the Quang Nam Pacification Project. During November 1965, membership on all of the committees of the council was expanded to include representatives of I Corps and the GVN as working members. The I Corps JCC started an Institutional Program which illustrated the importance of coordination. As the first step in the program, orphanages, schools, hospitals, sanitariums, ARVN dependents, and survivors of members of the Popular and Regional Forces were contacted to determine their requirements for living. The next step of the council was to discover the resources available within ICTZ and from outside to support the institutions, dependents, and survivors. The political and military organizations within I Corps Tactical Zone would use their resources and those available from outside the zone to fill the requirements. Coordination of this sort reduced overlapping efforts of support and brought relief to those whose needs had been overlooked.(14)

On 22 November 1965, the I Corps JCC took another forward step to assure coordinated programs of civic action and rural construction. The council formed a Joint Psychological Warfare/Civil Affairs Center whose mission was to develop themes and material of propaganda value, to prepare joint plans for psychological operations, and to organize audio-visual and civic action teams. The officer commanding the 3d Psychological Warfare Battalion of the ARVN was designated as the director of the center and the G-5, III MAF, was made the operations officer.

By November 1965, Marine Corps civic action was being synchronized with the Vietnamese struggle for survival through the medium of the I Corps JCC. HQ, III MAF became aware of the important 1966 plan for rural construction through the close liaison developed by the I Corps JCC and the directives received from ComUSMACV. Various younger Vietnamese leaders exemplified by Aspirant General Nguyen Duc Thang, Secretary of State for Rural Construction in October 1965, saw victory in the efforts of shock groups of young people trained at the national level in the paramilitary and political arts of bringing revolutionary change to the countryside. The groups would carry the war to the Viet Cong at the grass roots level in areas chosen as decisive by the government. One of the four priority, i.e., decisive, areas for rural construction in 1966, lay in the Da Nang area of Quang Nam Province. Marine Corps civic action to be most effective in the future would have to support Vietnamese rural construction in its latest form.

Against a background of improving coordination at the highest level, the Marine Corps battalions and squadrons carried out an imaginative program of civic action which remained enthusiastic but became more effective. In spite of a natural reticence on the part of the CG, I Corps, to place armed Vietnamese under the operational control of HQ, III MAF, the integration of Popular Forces in Marine Corps operations continued in November 1965. At the beginning of that month, the CG, I Corps, placed eight Popular Force platoons under Marine Corps direction in the Da Nang TAOR.(15) The Marine Corps began to train those platoons in small unit tactics and to integrate the units into the massive scheme of Marine Corps patrolling and ambushing.(16) Companies A and B, 1st Battalion, 3d Marines established training specifically in rifle marksmanship and scouting and patrolling in their areas, northwest of Da Nang. A Regional Forces platoon was also assigned to the 1st Battalion, 3d Marines and the battalion established a two week basic training camp for the Regional Forces in which personal hygiene, first aid, close order drill, rifle marksmanship, Vietnamese history, and English were stressed. The subjects taught revealed the qualitative weaknesses of both the Popular and Regional Forces. Personal hygiene, close order drill, and rifle marksmanship although requiring continuing stress were among the most basic military subjects.

In the Hue/Phu Bai area the tight integration of Marine Corps rifle squads within Popular Force platoons and the resulting Combined Action Companies was effective in expanding medical treatment, distribution of commodities, and other types of conventional and humanitarian civic action. The changing complexion of civic action, however, was shown on 29 November 1965 when a CAC squad ambushed a Viet Cong platoon and killed about 25 of its members.(17) The success of the CAC in furthering self-help projects among the villagers and providing security, led to the formation of additional CACs in the Da Nang and the Chu Lai TAORs. The importance of increasing the quality and encouraging the growth of the Popular Forces was difficult to exaggerate. The ARVN concentrated its attention in 1965 and 1966 on operations against the main forces of the Viet Cong; hence, security devolved on the Popular and the Regional Forces. Between main force operations and rural construction a security gap appeared which became the single most important factor in the slow progress of the war against the Viet Cong in 1966.(18) The importance of Marine Corps civic action and its dramatic expansion beyond the people-to-people concepts of spring 1965, was shown by the Combined Action Companies which were an attempt to close that gap.

Medical Assistance: Varying Techniques by November 1965

Medical treatments continued to be the mainstay of civic action towards the end of the year. The 1st Battalion, 3d Marines which had entered Vietnam in November 1965, took over the responsibility for the northwestern part of the Da Nang TAOR including the dispensary at Le My. In an effort to improve medical service by expanding it, the battalion changed the permanent dispensary at Le My to a mobile aid station which visited 11 different hamlets during each week. The mobile station remained in each hamlet for half a day. In the last few days of November 1965, using the mobile technique, the battalion medical team treated almost 500 civilians daily compared with approximately 250-300 daily at the permanent dispensary. The effort highlighted the complexities of civic action. For example, if the battalion were ordered to reinforce an operation against the main forces of the Viet Cong, the battalion medical team would be unable to provide so extensive a service. It was questionable, also, that the local Vietnamese authorities would ever have the transportation, personnel, or medical supplies to emulate the Marine Corps mobile teams.(19)

Farther south in the Da Nang TAOR, the 3d Battalion, 9th Marines operated in direct competition with a well developed Viet Cong infrastructure in a heavily populated area. The medical effort was a mobile one by necessity, but the peasants were reticent about receiving aid because of threats from the omnipresent Viet Cong. Whereas the battalion operating in the more securely pacified area around Le My treated approximately 5,000 Vietnamese civilians the harder pressed 3d Battalion, 9th Marines treated only 1,544 and most of these were children.(20) But the challenge in the south generated vigorous techniques for influencing an uncommitted population. On 19 November 1965, Company L coordinated the presentation of clothing and foodstuffs to 20 needy families in An Trach (1). The People's Action Team which operated in the hamlet area selected the families and Major Gia, the ARVN officer in charge of the Ngu Hanh Son Rural Construction Project, attended the presentation. Prior to the presentation an ARVN Psychological Warfare and Drama Team presented information and entertainment. Using techniques developed for the An Trach (1) presentation, i.e., Vietnamese determination of need, and the presence of Marines with local government officials, Company I of the same battalion coordinated the presentation of civic action supplies to needy peasants in Nhan Tho.(21)

Face-to-Face Persuasion

By the end of November 1965, Company K had developed a Civic Action/Psychological Warfare Team and employed it forward of the battalion's Forward Edge of the Battle Area on seven occasions. The company executive officer or the first sergeant acted as team leader. The composition of the team varied with the particular mission, but the team leader generally employed S-2 Section scouts, company and Medical Civic Action Program (MEDCAP) corpsmen, the battalion chaplain, several Marines especially interested in civic action, and possibly most important, an effective interpreter. The team would be transported by tank to a meeting place with a platoon patrol. Then, operating from a secure patrol base, the team would contact the local governing authority in a chosen area and arrange for medical assistance for the people. Simultaneously, Marines passed through the hamlet distributing psychological warfare material, searching homes, and distributing candy and/or other inexpensive supplies. The hamlet chief and the peasants who were felt to have information of intelligence value were separated from the rest of the villagers and interviewed privately.

The Commanding Officer, Company K described the technique as face-to-face persuasion; the vigorous program soon paid dividends. All members of the company were aware of the importance of correct and effective dealings with the rural population. On 15 November 1965, a patrol leader who had entered the hamlet of Bich Bac, nine miles south of Da Nang, interrogated a civilian who revealed the presence of several Viet Cong in the hamlet. The local resident explained that the Viet Cong were part of a larger force which operated west of Bich Bac. He elaborated that when Marine Corps patrols passed through the hamlets of Bich Bac and its western neighbor Thai Cam, the Viet Cong always fled on the trails leading southward from the hamlets.(22)

Using the information obtained from the face-to-face discussion of a well instructed patrol leader with a civilian who had decided to support the allies of his government, HQ, Company K spent several days planning an operation against the hamlets. Following careful planning, the company sent into the area a large patrol which purposely rested south of the hamlets and operated from there for the rest of the day. The patrol departed late in the afternoon but left behind south of the hamlets an ambush group which methodically and quietly moved into positions covering the southern trails from the hamlets. One small team spent approximately 18 hours within a few meters of a Vietnamese home without being detected. The next day the company sent another patrol into the hamlets from the east. Precisely as described by the friendly civilian the Viet Cong moved out towards the south. Walking swiftly and remaining extraordinarily well spaced, the Viet Cong blundered into the various ambush teams. Surprise was complete. The teams captured ten persons without a single shot being fired. The company commander had combined civic action and careful tactical planning to consummate an unusually successful ambush south of Bich Bac.(23)

A Growing Humanitarian Tradition

Throughout the Marine Corps TAORs individual efforts at civic action continued in what was becoming a growing Marine Corps tradition of humanitarianism. It would be unreasonable to say all or even most Marines were innately, positively oriented towards the individual type of civic action. A careful study by psychologists, military officers, statisticians, etc., would be required to establish the generality that all or most Marines were inherently compassionate ambassadors of good will. But, enough Marines were contributing special efforts on an individual basis to lend reality to the propaganda which proclaimed the beneficent purposes of the allies. Simultaneously the hard, purposeful civic action in support of security and rural construction was made more effective by the gentleness and commiseration of a substantial number of Marines. For example, in Company K alone of the 3d Battalion, 9th Marines more than 150 dollars had been spent by Marines on clothing for children in the area of Yen Ne (1) by the end of November 1965. The purchases had been an individual effort and they supported the well developed propaganda which emphasized that

Marines were friends of the Vietnamese people. In addition, a
medical corpsman from the company paid the annual tuition fee
enabling an 11-year old child to attend a Catholic girls'
school in Da Nang.(24) Examples of individual efforts similar
to those in Company K could be multiplied by the number of
Marine Corps companies throughout ICTZ.

The 3d Battalion, 9th Marines distributed representative
quantities and types of civic action materials also. Various
sources, including U. S. private and governmental organizations provided the basic materials in most cases. The battalion
distributed several hundred pounds of liquid and bar soap and
approximately 1,800 pounds of cornmeal and bulgar. The battalion also contributed in support of its civic action program
42 gallons of cooking oil and small quantities of salt, sugar,
candy, soft drink mix, and assorted toys. A private source in
the United States contributed a particularly humble offering--
50 rubber balls for children. Company I gave 25 pounds of
garbage daily during the month of November 1965 to the peasants
of Bo Mung for animal feed. The material distributed by the
battalion was moderate in quantity and disparate in usefulness,
e.g., rubber balls, garbage, wheat, and soft drink mix, but it
effectively supported medical assistance, psychological warfare,
face-to-face persuasion, and several hundred patrols and
ambushes. During November 1965, the battalion received an increased amount of intelligence from the Vietnamese peasants including that which led to the Bich Bac ambush and the identification or destruction of booby traps on five separate
occasions by the villagers at An Trach (1).(25) Finally, on
18 November 1965, a Viet Cong defected to the Regional Forces
703d Company, located within the battalion's TAOR, and explained
that a psychological warfare leaflet had been instrumental in
his defection. The leaflet was one of several hundred thousand
laboriously produced by the 3d Battalion, 9th Marines.

The End of the Year: December 1965

By December 1965, III MAF and its predecessor the 9th MEB
had operated for almost one year in Vietnam. Civic action had
initially been a weakly developed effort with limited command
emphasis. The complex process of landing and building up
strength had taken most of the Marine Corps time and effort.
Once the landing areas had been secured and logistics support
ensured, HQ, III MAF began to stress the expansion of its TAORs
in order to carry out its combat missions more effectively.
Each of the numerous expansions involved a change of positions
and a reconstruction of the FEBAs. General Walt placed heavy
emphasis on a well developed FEBA and a supporting Combat
Outpost Line. When the Marine Corps mission was expanded to
one of unilateral offensive action within its TAORs, the concentration of effort was on the detection and destruction of

main force Viet Cong units. The physical expansion of the TAORs in July 1965 also marked the beginning of more effective civic action. With the move into the more densely populated areas, competition began with the Viet Cong infrastructure in areas which neither side could afford to lose. The Headquarters of both FMFPac and III MAF became aware of the frustrating reality that successful actions against the main force of the Viet Cong would prevent the Republic's fall but victory would be achieved only with the success of the government's rural construction plan.

A Pattern of Civic Action

The following pattern of civic action supported the view that progress was slow at first, but as the importance of the struggle for the people was revealed, an increase in civic action began which only tapered off as III MAF reached the limits imposed by the necessary balance between military and civic action:

Activity	Time Periods and Approximate Strengths(26)			
	7-30May65 (13,000)	14Aug-30Sep65 (38,000)	1-31Oct65 (42,000)	1-31Dec65 (44,000)
Medical Aid (Civilians)	4,500	28,465	43,092	60,814
Food Distributed (pounds)		59,975	28,168	13,759
Clothing Distributed (pounds)		7,820	108,717	13,299
Small Unit Operations			5,662	7,208
Large Unit Operations			7	4
Enemy (KIA)	37	915	253	678

The most important gauges of activity were the numbers of civilians treated medically and small unit operations. These actions were dependent on the emphasis which commanders placed on them. The numbers of civilians treated and the number of small unit operations increased (44 and 28 percent respectively) even during the periods of October and December 1965 when the strength of III MAF remained almost stationary. In contrast, the distribution of food and clothing depended largely upon the receipt of the material from sources outside ICTZ and many cases within the continental limits of the United States. The uneven flow of material from the United States resulted in the uneven receipt and distribution in ICTZ. For example, the large quantity of 54.3 tons of clothing was received during October 1965, while two months later in December only 6.5 tons were received.(27)

By December 1965, III MAF had developed patterns of civic action which would continue through the following year. The I Corps JCC ensured coordination between the headquarters and directors of III MAF, I Corps, U. S. Operations Mission, and the U. S. private relief agencies. High level coordination remained effective although it was sensitive to political unrest within Vietnam. The working committees of the I Corps JCC focused the attention of the highest leadership on the problems of coordination at the hamlet/village level. But for numerous reasons coordination remained less effective at the lower levels. Coordination at the battalion level with the local government should have been all-encompassing. But the Marine Corps emphasized a coherent FEBA and a supporting Combat Outpost Line of Resistance to keep the main force of the Viet Cong at bay. In conjunction with the FEBA and the large unit operations conducted forward of it, HQ, III MAF placed emphasis on patrols and ambushes forward in the TAORs to suppress the guerrilla activity of the VC infrastructure. The heavy patrolling and the ubiquitous pressures of maintaining a cohesive FEBA/COPL and launching large unit operations gave the Marine Corps battalions little time for civic action in direct support of local government in the great area between the air installations and the forward combat positions.(28)

The Overriding Importance of Security
for Effective Civic Action

Lieutenant Colonel Ludwig of the 3d Battalion, 9th Marines had formed a joint security council for his battalion's TAOR in the summer of 1965, but this worthwhile experiment was not emulated by other battalions. Marine Corps civic action functioned as an effective services and supply effort in support of Vietnamese villagers who continued to be heavily influenced by the Viet Cong throughout the Marine Corps TAORs. In addition to the purely humanitarian motives, Marine Corps civic action had become a purposeful attempt to extract information from the rural population about the presence and movements of the Viet Cong. But in spite of an extraordinarily well developed medical aid program, a massive program of food supply, and the general tone of compassion and benevolence in Marine Corps operations, civic action remained defective in the most important particular--security.(29)

The Vietnamese peasant would not commit himself to the support of the GVN unless he and his family were adequately protected. Rural security had to take two forms. First the peasant had to be assured psychologically that the GVN and its powerful ally, the Marine Corps, were committed to a fight to a victorious conclusion. Second, the peasant had to be assured by the presence and execution of superior physical force that his chances of survival after exposing the presence of the Viet Cong or supporting the GVN/USMC were reasonable. Without giving these assurances to the peasantry, the Marine Corps could expect meager returns from its efforts in services and supply because of the continuing fear of retribution. Without security, the peasantry would remain an uncommitted mass of humanity among which the Viet Cong could continue to operate.

The importance of security was highlighted by the civic action program of the 3d Battalion, 7th Marines in the Chu Lai TAOR. This battalion had a particularly effective program of might be defined as "soft" civic action consisting largely of medical action and face-to-face contact with the people with extensive distribution of commodities.(30) Within the TAOR of the battalion, an outstanding hamlet chief came to light. Mr. Truong, the chief of Tri Binh (1) (see Map Number Two) was a fearless man who committed himself unequivocally to the Republican cause. Here was a man who was capable of winning the active support of his large hamlet and neighboring area close to Highway One in the southern part of the Chu Lai TAOR for the same Republican cause. He was a potential catalyst for a devasting reaction against Viet Cong influence in the Quang Tin district. On 3 December 1965, the medical aid team which visited Tri Binh (1) noted that he had posted several anti-Viet Cong signs in conspicuous locations in the hamlet. Near the entrance was a sign which stated, "Civilians and Soldiers Unite to Fight the Viet Cong." Another unusually provocative one stated, "What Have the Viet Cong Done for You--Nothing." The 3d Battalion, 7th Marines supported the chief with numerous medical visits and at the end of December helped in the construction of a pole for the Republican flag. The Marine Corps was pleased with the progress in Tri Binh (1). The people were happier and somewhat cleaner than in the neighboring areas, and sickness was decreasing. A patrol leader from Company L, remarked spontaneously to his gunnery sergeant after an initial visit to Mr. Truong's area: "You know, gunny, this is the first village we came into and found the people laughing and happy." It would be difficult to exaggerate the beneficial effects of a committed leader at the hamlet level; a way was opening up before the battalion which led to real control over part of Vietnam.

Unfortunately, the battalion report of 1 January 1966 read as follows:

> Mr. Truong, the hamlet chief of Tri Binh (1) was killed at approximately 310800 H /8 A.M. 31 December 1965 local time/ on the trail leading into Tri Binh (1). Four shots had been fired at him and one hit in the back of the head according to the assistant chief...footprints at 565985 showed that at least two murderers waited by the drainage ditch at 565985 to ambush the chief. The ID card had been removed from the...body...The villagers buried their chief at 311400 H.(31)

Fun and games II: here the boy of the photo at left is playing hopscotch. Lt Space instigated this affair also and is effectively combatting VC propaganda which portrays Marines as ruthless mercenaries. The young lad may soon have to be treated for exhaustion. (USMC A421637)

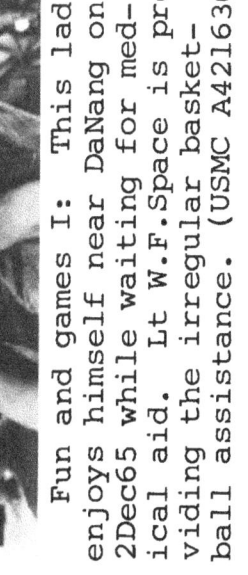

Fun and games I: This lad enjoys himself near DaNang on 2Dec65 while waiting for medical aid. Lt W.F.Space is providing the irregular basketball assistance. (USMC A421636)

With this brief passage the brave Mr. Truong passed into oblivion, but so did the chances of an effective civic action program for the 3d Battalion, 7th Marines. The chances of creating a rural population committed to the Republic in the battalion's TAOR receded into the distant future. Civic action in Tri Binh (1) again became the furnishing of medical assistance, food, clothing, candy, charms, all for a few bits of information snatched from terrified mouths. The flag continued to fly but without Mr. Truong it was a symbol of frustration instead of a rallying point for resistance against the terror.

What might have been done to protect the lion of Tri Binh (1) so that he could have led the peasants to a decisive annihilation of the Viet Cong in his area? A joint security council for the area probably would have revealed the isolated aspect of each hamlet and led to a communications network between the hamlets and between the local leaders and battalion headquarters. The joint security council could have dictated and enforced basic security measures by mutual agreement. For example, Mr. Truong was alone and unarmed when he was assassinated. As a committed hamlet chief, he should have been protected by a 24-hour guard of trusted men, preferably blood relations. This guard would have served almost naturally as the nucleus for a hamlet self-defense force. None of these measures would have guaranteed Mr. Truong's life. But the Viet Cong would have had an immensely more difficult task of assassination than having a few political killers loll along the trail into Tri Binh (1) and almost casually dispatch the unarmed and unaccompanied hamlet chief.(32)

Security and the Quang Nam Pacification Project:
December 1965

In the Da Nang area, the Quang Nam Pacification Project took a dramatic turn for the worse. The effort was designed to reestablish government control in the densely populated area south of Da Nang and was the major rural construction effort in the ICTZ. The importance of the effort was based on the following factor: Da Nang, with its extensive resources in port and communications facilities, repair shops, machine tools, etc., and surrounding air installations was the hub of Republican activity in the north. But the Viet Cong infrastructure was entrenched from the southern outskirts of the port outward into the countryside and served as an opposing axis for insurgent operations in ICTZ. The powerful Viet Cong influence also carried with it the danger of serving as a springboard for a successful raid against Da Nang in the event of any shift of Allied strength out of the area. As a result, the nine villages south of Da Nang had been designated as one of four national priority areas for rural construction. The program had begun in November and immediately ran into stiff Viet Cong resistance. The Viet Cong were forced to react because the center of their strength lay not in the main force units in the uninhabited hills but in the political infrastructure and supporting guerrilla fighters of the rich lowlands. The Viet Cong recognized the Quang Nam Pacification Project as a crucial development. Years of patient, bedrock organizing were threatened by the government campaign.

Marine Corps civic action was clustered rather closely around Da Nang (see Map Number One for a representative day of Marine Corps activity in the Da Nang TAOR) and served as a natural adjunct to the activities of the Vietnamese Rural Construction Cadres of the People's Action Teams. Marine Corps medical assistance and the distribution of food and clothing were a form of rural construction themselves. A calculated blending of civic action and the formal Vietnamese program of rural construction might have had decisive results. But from the beginning the Vietnamese effort lacked satisfactory security forces; and the orientation of the Marine Corps towards combat forward in the TAORs prevented a conclusive reinforcing of the rural construction program by III MAF. The ARVN provided only a penny packet security force; and the end result was that the program foundered on the rocks of inadequate security.(33)

The Viet Cong broke the back of the campaign during the period 21-28 December 1965. Marine Corps civic action was especially active during this time, and the campaign area lay completely within the Marine Corps TAOR. But the activity was in the soft form of the distribution of commodities and the provision of services rather than in the hard form of a security program wherein services and commodities were supporting appendages rather than the central issue. The Vietnamese operators of the rural construction program were largely members of the People's Action Teams sent into the area. These political units had only a limited capability of self-defense although they could be called paramilitary organizations as well as political. They existed primarily, however, to lead the rural population in self-help projects of a peaceful political and economic nature in areas where the Viet Cong guerrilla fighters had been eliminated.(34) The campaign began with difficulties in supply, coordination, and changes of leadership, and progress during the first two months was only moderate. But the Viet Cong feared any progress and was painfully aware of the importance of its infrastructure in the Da Nang area.

On 21 December 1965, the Viet Cong launched several attacks specifically against the rural construction program and ominously maneuvered through the area. At 0300, the People's Action Team at 016660 (see Map Number One which has a 10,000 meter grid square on it and read to the right 016, and upwards 660) was hit by a Viet Cong guerrilla force which killed four PAT members and carried off two automatic weapons.

Fifteen minutes prior to this strike, the Communists had launched a mortar attack against campaign headquarters at 011661. Then, at 0315 a contact was made by the 594th Regional Forces Company with a group of Viet Cong maneuvering through the campaign area; the Regional Forces killed three of the enemy. On the afternoon of the same day, the Viet Cong launched a sharp attack against the 593d Regional Forces Company, a unit whose specific mission was to protect the PATs. The Viet Cong killed seven of the Regional Forces as well as capturing three automatic weapons and two AN/PRC-10 radios (medium range radios carried on packs).(35)

Instead of reinforcing the campaign area with adequate security forces, the GVN replaced the campaign chief on 24 December 1965 with an ARVN regimental commander who moved the campaign headquarters and required precious days to become an effective leader in the new assignment. Even more important, the direct leadership of the PATs devolved on no single assistant to the new chief, and rural construction began to grind to a halt because of the lack of security and leadership. The Viet Cong, however, were far from finished with their activity. At 1700 on 28 December 1965, at 037704, a sniper deliberately picked out and killed a member of a PAT. Later on the same day, at 1930, the People's Action Team at 041721 was attacked by the Viet Cong who killed two team members and wounded a third. Approximately two weeks after these events, Lieutenant Colonel Loc, the new rural construction chief, was replaced by yet another man. The Viet Cong in a series of purposeful attacks had set back progress in the Quang Nam Pacification Project to an indeterminate future date.(36)

Marine Corps "Power"

Security was the most important part of any civic action program carried out by the Marine Corps which was intended either to support rural construction or to gain the willing support of the populace. It was so basic a part of successful civic action that in many cases it was overlooked as the indispensable factor in progress towards a committed Vietnamese population. As far in the past as May 1965, Lieutenant Colonel Clement had seen that in order to be in control of his TAOR, he would have to fight his battle within the hardcore Viet Cong village complex of Le My. He was fortunate in his location. His battalion's TAOR and mission coincided in such a way that the rifle companies were available for security throughout the village complex. Faced with an effective effort to destroy its infrastructure, the Viet Cong was forced to fight to maintain its influence within Le My. But the rifle companies and a reviving Popular Force organization were too strong for the Viet Cong and Le My village fell under the control of the Republican government. The neighboring village chief, Mr. Tac-Bac of Hoa Thanh, expressed his feelings about the civic action of the 2d Battalion, 3d Marines in a manner which stood out like a beacon in expressing what was important about the battalion's activities:

> We the people of Northwest Hoa Vang District wish to express our feelings toward...the 2d Battalion, 3rd Marines who...are now acting in our Northwest Zone.... We are very pleased with the battalion. We believe in US Marine Corps power. /The Marine Corps/ came to our country, landed, and cleared our zone of Viet Cong. Then with its power it defended and held our zone, keeping the Viet Cong from invading us...To present an example of the fighting power and will of the American Government, the Viet Cong in Hoa Lac /Le My/ village have all been flushed out...the Viet Cong have not dared come back to harrass us any more...Also we are very happy because you helped us rebuild our bridges in Hoa Lac...And we are very thankful towards your doctors.(37)

Mr. Tac-Bac's letter was a guide to successful civic action in Vietnam. The guide emphasized two vital points. First, ensure the security of any area in which successful civic action was contemplated. Then, support the reviving local government in projects chosen by that government. By December 1965, the Combined Action Company of the 3d Battalion, 4th Marines in the Hue/Phu Bai area struck an ideal balance between hard and soft civic action, or effective security and distribution of services and supplies. Marine rifle squads actually lived with the Popular Force platoons in Vietnamese hamlets and ensured the domination of the countryside by fire and physical presence. Communications between the CAC and the battalion Combat Operations Center ensured the use of most of the weapons in the Marine Corps armory against the Viet Cong. The closeness of the Marine rifle squad to the villagers resulted in an unusually effective medical program and the provision of various bits of assistance to the local government officials. Probably though, the rapport which developed between the Marine rifle squads and the Popular Forces and villagers was based on the supreme camarderie of sharing real danger and overcoming it. By the time the 3d Battalion, 4th Marines left Hue/Phu Bai, on 22 December 1965, a close bond had been forged between the Marines and the Vietnamese villagers. "The people were sad and heartbroken" and they lined "the road for three hundred meters watching...the Marines leave. The Marines noted that many of the people were crying...."(38)

By the end of the first calendar year for major Marine Corps forces in Vietnam, other shreds of evidence supported the importance of security for civic action. Early in December 1965, several Marine Corps units contributed to a sweep of the Phong Bac area located only a few thousand meters south of the

Da Nang Airbase and close to Route One. Phong Bac had been well within the Marine Corps TAOR for many months and had been the object of civic action efforts by several Marine Corps units. The 3d Motor Transport, 3d Tank, and 1st Amphibian Tractor Battalions had carried on civic action programs in the hamlet which had become a saturated area for medical service and the distribution of commodities (see Map Number One for a representative day of civic action in the Da Nang TAOR). During the sweep, about 160 villagers were interrogated concerning Viet Cong activities in the area. The peasants' lingering fear of the Viet Cong was sharply etched in the report of the questioning. The 3d Tank Battalion's report noted that the "villagers seemed to be grateful for our concern over their safety."(39)

The villagers had good reason for concern over their safety. Although retribution took a while, the Viet Cong managed to extract it from people who had consorted with their own government and its allies. The report of the 3d Tank Battalion on 2 December 1965 took on an ominous cast when set next to the following: "25 January 1966. The Battalion CAO talked to the various people of Phong Bac concerning the assassination of Nguyen Tang, youth director of Hoa Tho Village /which included Phong Bac/." From the information received, the Youth Director was evidently taken from his home near Phong Bac by a Viet Cong assassination squad which led him to Route One, several hundred meters above the Hoa Tho Village headquarters and shot him. The 3d Tank Battalion report concluded with the masterful understatement that "this /murder/ will create serious difficulties in the village."(40)

Farther south, in the Chu Lai TAOR, the Vietnamese also sought protection from the Viet Cong and were grateful for Marine Corps security. The peasants of Nuoc Man hamlet in the area of responsibility of the 3d Battalion, 7th Marines spontaneously carried out a people-to-people project of their own. In order to provide shelter for Marines located near the hamlet, they built a grass and bamboo building which was completed on 2 December 1965. The villagers then donated the building specifically to the Marines who were manning the nearby security outpost. One month later in the TAOR of the 1st Battalion, 4th Marines, Company D conducted a survey in the Ky Xuan village complex (487103) to gather information on the people's reaction to the Marine Corps civic action program. The sweep was similar to the one conducted by the 3d Tank Battalion at Phong Bac in the Da Nang TAOR and revealed the same ominous concern of the peasants for their lives. "The villagers of Ky Xuan felt that they /were_/ safe from the Viet Cong during the day but still not at night. They wanted Marines or some troops to stay in the village at all times."(41) The peasants also wanted their children to go to school and felt that the Marine Corps medical assistance was helpful. But the primary concern of the peasants was security.

Christmas 1965: "Peace on Earth, Good Will Towards Man"

The Christmas season presented opportunities for increased contact between Marines and the local population. Christmas parties for children of neighboring hamlets, refugee centers, orphanages, and hospitals burgeoned and reinforced the normal medical assistance and distribution of commodities. The 1st Amphibian Tractor Battalion originated an imaginative program using its enormous LVTP-5s (Landing Vehicle Tracked, Personnel, Model Number 5). The battalion painted one of the vehicles white, placed a Santa Claus, sled, reindeer, and a Christmas tree on top and painted various Christmas designs around the LVTP-5. The slogan, "Peace on Earth, Good Will Toward Man," was painted on both sides of the vehicle in Vietnamese, and the LVT was outfitted with a sound system that played Christmans carols continuously while the vehicle was on the move.(42)

On 23 December 1965, the white LVT went to the Sampan Community of Khue Trung (036757) where Santa Claus distributed candy and toys to approximately 200 children of that unusual floating community. During the next two days, Santa continued his benevolent rounds, making one trip through downtown Da Nang to Marble Mountain on 24 December, and another trip through Hoa Yen (990770) and the Hoa Cam Training Center for Popular Forces (985718) on Christmas Day. During the three days of his travels, the hard-working Santa Claus distributed about 500 pounds of candy to approximately 2,500 children. Adults as well as children "were overjoyed at seeing Santa and his sleigh and reindeer." The inscription on the sides of the LVT --Peace on Earth, Good Will Toward Man--was also well received by a violence-weary population.(43)

Clothes for little boys: Vietnamese children were generally poorly protected from ground and weather. Punctures of the feet and infestation by worms were by-products of missing foot wear. The danger of overexposure to the sun was great and the early morning chill turned colds into pneumonia amongst scantily-clad children. (USMC A184605)

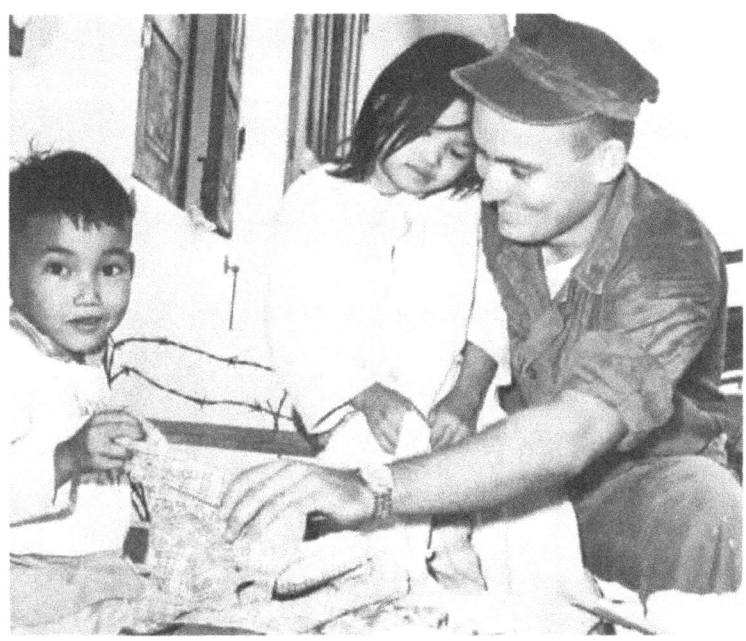

Clothes for little girls (and boys): lightweight clothes were welcomed by the needy in Vietnam. These were received from U.S. charity and are being presented by Sgt Kurt L. Cordes to two relaxed youngsters. In a parallel program the Marine Reserve and CARE contributed sewing kits and cloth which helped to balance charity with self-help. 1966 (USMC A421367)

Chapter VII

A New Calendar Year:
Patterns of Civic Action in January-March 1966

The new year, 1966, opened with the rural construction campaign of the GVN stalled in the Ngu Hanh Son area, south of Da Nang. The Viet Cong attacks of 21-28 December 1965 had forced a reorganization of the program. The GVN had originally scheduled the campaign to be completed by 31 December 1965, but early in January 1966, Major Nhat, the "current pacification chief," who had replaced Lieutenant Colonel Loc, noted that a new three-phase concept was in effect for rural construction in the area of the nine villages. The GVN scheduled five of the villages in the area for pacification during April 1966. Major Nhat prepared for the future effort by reorganizing the civilian teams which lacked a clear-cut chain of command. But he was unable to reinforce the security forces enough to assure the safety of the People's Action Teams. Security forces comprised an understrength battalion of the Regional Forces, four platoons of Popular Forces, and a single company of the ARVN. The 2d Battalion, 9th Marines was to assist in providing security in the forward fringe of the rural construction area. But the Marine Corps and the ARVN continued to focus most of their attention on the main force of the Viet Cong.(1)

Security within the Marine Corps TAOR and behind the FEBA remained inadequate to support the Vietnamese rural construction effort. The Vietnamese government lost its initial, driving interest in the campaign and the ARVN continued to neglect the effort in any calculations of the allotment of resources. For example, the single ARVN company supporting the campaign was no more than a token force and was hard-pressed to provide for the security of the campaign headquarters. In the meantime, during the last four months of 1965, the national government at Saigon had begun to plan for rural construction in 1966. The failures of 1965 and the gains of the Viet Cong from 1963-1965 dictated more emphasis on winning the peasantry at the hamlet level and changing the bland term rural construction. The words revolutionary development (RD) began to be used for the better-coordinated 1966 program in place of the former uninspired terminology.(2) In February 1966, the national government revived its interest in winning the Quang Nam peasantry by political, social, and economic action, and renamed the Quang Nam Pacification Project area the Revolutionary Development National Priority Area of I Corps. But the GVN decided to complete Phase I of the new program during April 1966, i.e., in the indeterminate future. Civil strife, however, wracked the ICTZ during the months of March-May 1966 and cancelled any efforts at revolutionary development in the Ngu Hanh Son area. A policy of drift had set in after the Viet Cong attacks of late December 1965. The policy resulted from the lack of resources to protect the political teams and set back progress in the campaign beyond the middle of 1966.

Nevertheless, HQ, III MAF cooperated with the GVN on certain lesser projects around Da Nang short of an area campaign. Planning began on 19 January 1966 for the construction of the Cam Ne/Yen Ne New Life Hamlet. The plans for the hamlet were well coordinated; planners included the Quang Nam Province Chief, Commanding Officer, Ninth Marines, G-5, III MAF, and the Provincial Representative of USAID. The Vietnamese government was firmly in control of the project but needed bits and pieces of Marine Corps assistance. The Vietnamese required a TD-18 type earth moving tractor for leveling the proposed site. After the original coordinating meeting the G-5, 3d Marine Division and the Division Engineer took up the precise details of support.(3) This important project, which actually formed one small part of the Quang Nam Pacification Project, went forward in fits and starts. The Vietnamese officials had a difficult time in choosing a location for the hamlet; the original site which included part of a cemetery proved unacceptable to the future inhabitants. They had come to believe that the past death of so many people near the site was an unfavorable omen for the future. The Marine Corps played its proper civic action role in this affair. It faithfully supported the GVN with engineer equipment and patiently relocated its equipment after the tractor operators had begun work on the superstition-laden first site.

Operation MALLARD:
Civic Action in Support of Large Unit Operations

Southwest of the Da Nang TAOR, and early in January 1966, the 3d Marines conducted Operation MALLARD, a search and destroy mission in an area which provided an ideal testing ground for civic action during a large unit tactical operation. The area was densely populated and had been under Viet Cong control for two years. Several challenges to civic action existed. The Marine Corps would have to subject a large population to an intense, short-term civic action program; and, voluntary refugees would have to be retrieved. The 3d Marines gathered a vast quantity of food, MEDCAP supplies, clothing, soap, and candy. The supplies were placed in the Logistics Support Area (LSA) for the operation and were available at the call of the commander. HQ, 3d Marines directed its subordinate units to establish civilian collection points. These were locations where the civilians would be relatively safe from the hazards of formal combat and where they would not interfere with the tactical maneuver. The supplies available on call at the LSA were used to care for the civilians who were temporarily separated from their homes, food supplies, cooking facilities, etc., and to support a combined civic action and psychological warfare effort which would influence the population favorably towards the GVN. Civilians at the collection points who requested to leave the areas controlled by the Viet Cong were transported to the GVN district headquarters to begin a new life.(4)

The Vietnamese peasants responded in the usual favorable way to relief from the harsh control of the Viet Cong. Significant numbers stated that they were tired of the war and wished to escape the rigors of Viet Cong domination. The 3d Marines exploited the anticipated unrest with aerial broadcasts urging the people to leave their homes for resettlement in government-controlled areas. Approximately 1,000 civilians responded to the call in spite of the challenge of resettlement.(5)

The operation revealed another reason for the dissatisfaction of the peasantry besides ruthless administration. The Viet Cong were exploiting the entire area as a food supply and storage area. Enormous quantities of rice had been taken from the peasantry to support the Viet Cong apparatus not only for local guerrillas, but also for larger units operating in distant areas. The 3d Marines uncovered more than 35 tons of hidden rice and transported it to the Dai Loc district headquarters for government use. The favorable psychological impact of 35 tons of rice arriving at the district headquarters for distribution by the local government was a major victory for Marine Corps civic action.(6)

Operations of the I Corps JCC

During and after Operation MALLARD, at the highest level of civic action coordination, the I Corps JCC concentrated on plans for the distribution of the supplies received through the Christmas collection campaign in the United States. Americans contributed supplies through the American Christmas Trucks and Trains program (ACTT) for the needy in Vietnam. The material had to be distributed efficiently and fairly throughout the ICTZ. The I Corps Joint Coordinating Council was ideally suited to coordinate the distribution, and the Commodities Distribution Committee handled the manifold details. Those details provided an insight into the complexities of the Vietnamese situation and the problems of inertia at the various levels of government. Upon the recommendation of the committee, the I Corps JCC set up province-level Commodities Distribution Committees to estimate province needs in accordance with the following priorities system:(7)

1. Needy families in newly pacified hamlets.
2. Refugees and ralliers (VC defectors) in resettlement centers.

3. Popular Force members and their families.
4. Widows and survivors of armed forces personnel.
5. Orphanages and hospitals.

These priorities also served as a guide for concentration of effort in the provision of services and the distribution of commodities for civic action programs at any level of command in Vietnam throughout the year.

United States and Vietnamese personnel who were assigned the task of inventorying the ACTT commodities did not complete it until March 1966. By that time the tactical units and the provincial committee had made known their requirements and the I Corps JCC Commodities Distribution Committee coordinated the issue of the Christmas donations using transportation contributed by the military units and civilian agencies. The military commanders in ICTZ agreed through the JCC to give 20 percent of the commodities to the tactical units and to divide the remainder among the Vietnamese civilian authorities in the five provinces.(8)

Civic Action Pattern of Activity: January 1966

By January 1966, Marine Corps civic action had settled into an effective and well defined pattern. Important but unusual projects like the receipt of ACTT supplies were coordinated by the I Corps JCC. In the more characteristic day-to-day civic action, the medical assistance program was extraordinarily well-developed and the tendency was towards either permanent fixed dispensaries or mobile service operating on a regular schedule. Marines distributed the following types of supplies in large quantities and often in conjunction with medical services: food, clothing, soap, CARE school kits (see Appendix One), and candy. Marines assisted Vietnamese in construction projects which fell into the pattern of repairs on bridges and culverts and the construction of schoolrooms and dispensaries. The construction projects were simple, restrained, and oriented toward self-help on the part of the Vietnamese. Psychological warfare had been combined with civic action in many Marine Corps units by January 1966 under the direction of either a G-5 or a Civil Affairs Officer. Civic action visits were commonly combined with the distribution of propaganda leaflets, drama and cinema presentations, and loudspeaker broadcasts.(9)

The Growing Bond Between Civic Action and Psychological Warfare

The Vietnamese Open Arms Amnesty Program (its Vietnamese designation, Chieu Hoi) helped to focus Marine Corps civic action and psychological warfare on an important part of Vietnamese revolutionary development--the encouragement of Viet Cong to defect to the government side. The Diem government had introduced Chieu Hoi in March 1963 as an effort parallel with the strategic hamlet concept of the time. The open arms campaign was based on the successful policy of the Philippines' Defense Minister Magsaysay in encouraging the defection of Huks. Magsaysay resettled them on land of their own with equipment and supplies for farming. "In effect he made it both easy and attractive to become loyal to the government."(10)

The Vietnamese government had made elaborate plans for Chieu Hoi late in 1963, but the coup in November 1963, which overthrew Diem, dislocated the program. Without firm direction, the program drifted throughout 1964. In 1965, however, with the arrival of major U. S. ground forces and the increase in government morale, the program became effective. Problems remained in the indoctrination of officials and infantrymen who received ralliers and in the provisions for resettlement; but, the rising numbers of defectors signalled important successes. "After mid-1965, an average of 1,000 returnees each month /came/ to the government side; and the numbers for January (1,672) and February (2,011) of 1966 broke previous monthly records."(11)

Psychological warfare themes by the turn of 1966 were closely tied to Vietnamese revolutionary development.(12) The following themes were the key ones in mid-January 1966 and illustrated the importance of Marine Corps civic action and Vietnamese revolutionary development in the war: (1) the Viet Cong are losing the war, (2) the GVN has the resources to govern the people best, (3) the GVN can provide a more abundant life than the Viet Cong, (4) the Viet Cong are the real enemies of the people, and (5) surrender and be received with open arms.(13) The themes supported the allied war effort yet they were more closely associated with revolutionary development and civic action than formal combat.

The Marine Corps emphasized the five themes during Operation MALLARD (11-17 January 1966) but towards the end of the month introduced two others to support an effort of indoctrination during the celebration of the lunar new year by the Vietnamese. The celebration, known as Tet Nguyen Dan (TET) formally extended from 21-23 January 1966 but actually included about 12 days of activity.(14) During TET, in accordance with social custom, the Vietnamese reduced business activity and in some areas even raised prohibitions against receiving medical attention. The Vietnamese envisioned TET as a time of joyous family gatherings with games and feasting as well as the ritual associated with the veneration of the family ancestors.(15) Marine Corps psychological warfare concentrated on the burden placed on the people by the Viet Cong and especially the separation of family members and the taxes and physical terror. Finally, the second fresh theme reminded the Viet Cong themselves of their own hardships during TET with particular emphasis on broken family ties.(16)

Emphasis on Medical Assistance

During January 1966, medical assistance continued to be the most important part of civic action. Marines and Navy corpsmen treated a sharply reduced number of civilians as a result of the TET celebrations, but in spite of the four-day suspension of medical assistance, Marine Corps units treated 56,000 people for medical and dental ailments. A total of 40 MEDCAP teams provided the assistance at 120 different locations. The most common ailment treated was skin infection especially in the scalp area. Headaches and complaints of the upper respiratory tract were the next most common ailments. Fifty-four percent of the Vietnamese assisted medically were treated for these three general afflictions.(17) The afflictions revealed the unsophisticated nature of the medical service in which children received most of the treatments with adult females and males following in that order. The bulk of the MEDCAP program consisted of quick and simple treatment for a multitude of scantily-clad and poorly attended children.(18)

The distribution of treatments revealed the following pattern. The 3d Marine Division with most of the Marines carried out the bulk of the medical assistance, treating more than 38,000 civilians. The 1st Marine Air Wing assisted approximately 2,000 civilians and the Force Logistics Support Group treated most of the remaining 16,000 citizens.(19) The thin effort of the air wing deserved examination because the static nature of the air installations favored a well-developed program. For example, a fixed operating area was important for the continuity of medical treatment and favored the build up of a large clientele. Part of the explanation for the paucity of medical treatment in the air wing lay in the general coincidence of civic action areas of responsibilities with TAORs. The TAORs of the battalions of the 3d Marine Division abutted on the perimeters of the air installations; and, the battalions carried out civic as well as combat action within their TAORs. The result was that little territory remained for the air wing in which to carry on civic action programs except on a shared basis with a neighboring battalion. The enormous maintenance and air control effort required to keep both the fixed wing and helicopter aircraft flying was another factor which drastically reduced civic action in the air wing.

Civic Action Programs Rivaling Medical Assistance by January 1966

Although medical assistance remained the single most important part of civic action, several other programs were beginning to rival it in importance. The Catholic Relief Service, a private relief society, made an impressive effort in January 1966, delivering the huge quantity of 430,000 pounds of rolled wheat to units of III MAF. Project HANDCLASP, a combined effort of the naval service and a multitude of private relief donors in the United States, delivered through Navy and Marine Corps transportation approximately 63,000 pounds of miscellaneous basic commodities e.g., clothing, food, drugs, etc.. The special Christmas program carried on in the United States for Vietnamese relief and called American Christmas Trains and Trucks delivered 300 measurement tons (one measurement ton was the equivalent of 40 cubic feet of cargo space) of commodities to Vietnam in January. The Marine Corps Reserve Civic Action Fund for Vietnam operating through CARE channels delivered 3,666 school kits to III MAF as well as large quantities of other kinds of self-help kits, e.g., textile, woodworking, and midwifery (see Appendix One).(20) The reserve fund concentrated on improving rural education while the CRS was the major contributor of food.

Early in January 1966, the 1st Battalion, 7th Marines, in the Chu Lai area launched an intensive civic action program in the Vinh An-Hai Ninh complex of hamlets (see Map Number Two) at the mouth of the Tra Bong River. The three hamlets, which were scheduled for revolutionary development by the Vietnamese with Marine Corps assistance, were a scant 6,000 meters from the southern edge of the air installation at Chu Lai. But no Vietnamese government had existed in them for the two years since the overthrow of the Diem regime late in 1963. No schools functioned and no medical assistance was available to the villagers. The hamlets served the Viet Cong as a convenient way station for movements into the Chu Lai area from the south and east. On 29 December 1965, Company A moved into the hamlets, established a permanent patrol base, and began to work closely with a 25-man People's Action Team.

While the People's Action Team ferreted out the Viet Cong infrastructure and established local government, Company A concentrated on medical assistance and the improvement of hygiene. The Marine rifle company provided saturation security for both its own civic action and Vietnamese revolutionary development, and as a result, progress was rapid. After a few days, the PAT discovered a former school teacher and soon after reopened a primary school. The people of the hamlets selected officials in elections organized by the PAT. Company A in close coordination with the political team began to organize a Popular Force unit. The people of the hamlets responded warmly to the program and were relieved at being withdrawn from Viet Cong control. The village chief of the three hamlets proved to be an aggressive leader who concentrated on developing an effective Popular Force unit for the defense of his flock.(21)

What were the lessons of the rapid progress in Vinh An-Hai Ninh? Probably most important was the hard fact that the people feared and hated the Viet Cong. Once the people were assured of protection and were reorganized by the Republican Vietnamese they eagerly, almost pathetically, clutched at the opportunity to live productive lives in the Republic. The swiftness and ease with which the Vietnamese in the Vinh An-Hai Ninh area were returned to the government camp, proved the hatred of the villagers for the Viet Cong. Additionally, Company A provided blanket-like security in the limited area of the three hamlets and the combination of Marine Corps "power" and Vietnamese revolutionary development quickly reestablished a community responsive to the Republican will. The hold of the Viet Cong over the villagers had been based on psychological and physical fear and an enormous hostage system. The main force of the Viet Cong held the young fighters as hostages from their families while simultaneously the clandestine infrastructure held families as hostages from the fighters in the main force. But the Viet Cong hold over the countryside lapsed with the institution of security and the destruction of the infrastructure. Conversely, however, a loyal Republican peasantry could be terrorized back into submission to the Viet Cong practically overnight.(22)

Vietnamese New Year: 20-23 January 1966

On 19 January 1966, the Civil Affairs Officer of the 1st Battalion, 7th Marines, returned the PAT operating with Company A to Vinh Son for the celebration of TET. Civic action was a never-ending task and while in Binh Son the CAO turned over 16,000 dollars (VN) to Father Diek of the Catholic Refugee Center for the care of 40 orphans. TET officially began at 1200 20 January 1966 and III MAF carried out a drastic reduction of civic action on that day. But while III MAF reduced medical assistance to negligible proportions and restricted the distribution of the normal commodities, it increased face-to-face contacts with the Vietnamese people. The Marine Corps emphasized small cash gifts in envelopes for children; and numerous Marines and Vietnamese civilians met for the first time during the general distribution of the envelopes to the children.(23) Additionally, many local government officials and private citizens extended invitations to Marines to participate in the holiday festivities.

Early on the morning of 21 January 1966, Mr. Dien, the hamlet chief of Tri Binh (1) (see Map Number Two) and the man who had replaced the ill-fated Mr. Truong, extended a general invitation to the 3d Battalion, 7th Marines, to celebrate TET

English classes: by the end of 1965, English classes burgeoned in the Marine TAORs. The Vietnamese people showed deep interest, and adults as well as children enrolled in large numbers. PFC Patrick Moore instructs in this scene in January 1966. (USMC A186596)

in his hamlet. Five officers and 46 men represented the Marine Corps in what turned out to be an extraordinarily successful affair. Mr. Dien initiated the celebration with sound political sense by reading messages from the Province and District Chiefs wishing the villagers a prosperous and happy new year. After the messages has been read, Mr. Dien raised the Republican flag over the hamlet. Then he explained to the villagers that five months ago Tri-Binh (1) had been poor, but since that time the Marine Corps had come to the assistance of the hamlet with medical treatment, food, and clothing. The chief emphasized that the Marines had helped the villagers to improve themselves. Finally, he picked up the ubiquitous theme of security and stated that he was not afraid and would work to improve Tri-Binh (1) even though the Viet Cong had killed the former chief, Mr. Truong.(24)

The villagers and Marines enjoyed each other's company so much on 21 January 1966, that the villagers extended an invitation for the following day. The visiting Marines enjoyed themselves even more on 22 January and at 2230 were still in the hamlet playing the Vietnamese version of bingo. At that time the village elders divided the Marines into groups of twos and threes and then took them to their respective homes where Marines and Vietnamese participated in an extensive banquet. "The villagers were excited and happy that the Marines were able to participate in TET" and requested that the Marines return for a third day of holiday revelry. The success of the face-to-face social activity at Tri-Binh (1) was based on several factors. The hamlet chief vigorously courted the Marine Corps for his hamlet. The Civil Affairs Officers of the 3d Battalion, 7th Marines, realized the privilege of social interaction with the villagers on their New Year's holiday and the beneficial impact of about 50 well-instructed Marines on the peasants. Finally, Chief Dien was a paragon of earthy peasant guile--50 Marines alert for a possible Viet Cong incident made Tri Binh (1) the most secure hamlet in the Chu Lai area during TET.(25)

In the TAOR of the 1st Battalion, 7th Marines, the villagers of the Vinh An-Hai Ninh area celebrated TET with two significant ceremonies. First, they planned and carried out an elaborate symbolic ambush of the Viet Cong. Apparently using the principles of homeopathic magic, the villagers sought to ensure a successful defense against their former harsh masters. In addition to the ambush, the villagers conducted a flag raising ceremony and committed themselves overtly to the Republican cause. These activities originated with the villagers; the People's Action Teams assigned to the village for Revolutionary Development had departed to celebrate TET in its own area around Binh Son.(26) Farther north, in the Da Nang TAOR, the 2d Battalion, 9th Marines carried on an active Civic Action Program concentrating on the local school at Duong Son (3) (999670). The villagers were anxious to get their school in operation notwithstanding TET. As a result, the Marines presented CARE school and woodworking kits, and desks of their own making to the people and also treated patients at the battalion aid station.(27) At Hue/Phu Bai, the Vietnamese registered complete acceptance of the Marine Corps members of the CAC during TET. In one of the villages, the peasants invited members of the Marine rifle squad of the combined action platoon into more than fifty different homes for games and banquets.(28)

A Representative Day of Civic Action

January 1966 was a reasonable month to take stock of Marine Corps Civic Action in Vietnam in the general sense, for example, of representative activity on a particular day. The Marine Corps had been ashore in strength for almost a year and civic action had developed patterns which would be reflected on a carefully chosen day. On 15 January 1966, the Marine Corps operated in a representative way for the Vietnamese war, and civic action was not affected by unusual events like Christmas, TET, etc. Maps One, Two, and Three show Marine Corps civic action at work in the three TAORs. The Marine Corps units concentrated on medical assistance (red circles) but distributed commodities (blue circles) in significant quantities at numerous locations. Marines also assisted the Vietnamese in construction projects (green circles) which varied in complexity from the building of a schoolroom or a children's hospital to the repair of a culvert on a primitive road.(29) Dr. A. R. Frankle, Assistant Civil Affairs Officer, 3d Engineer Battalion pressed hard for a dispensary at Da Son and the Battalion technical personnel pooled their talents to produce a complex civil engineering effort in his support.(30)

The units of III MAF carried out most of their civic action close to the defensive centers of the TAOR, i.e., the air installations. Most of the ground units which supported the infantry battalions were located near the air installations. The air units themselves and the infantry battalions which manned the immediate perimeters were clustered in and around the bases. In the Da Nang area in particular, a pattern of saturation in civic action had grown up by the middle of January 1966. The battalions close to the base concentrated vigorously on the two hamlets of Phong Bac and Da Son. These hamlets became saturated with civic action while farther out in the TAOR in the vast areas controlled by the infantry battalions, civic action was spread more thinly. The pattern of action on the maps pointed to an enlargement of the civic action areas of responsibility of the supporting battalions and the air units to prevent an unfair distribution of services and commodities. The units of the 1st Marine Air Wing were especially restricted in their civic action programs by both the protecting and the neighboring ground units.

Unexpected Reinforcements

In February 1966, III MAF discovered unexpected reinforcements for civic action. The 3d Marine Division Band and Drum and Bugle Corps played at a series of public events and excited enthusiastic, favorable response. Warrant Officer William E. Black, director of the band (and the drum and bugle corps), presented one of the highlights of civic action in the TAOR of the 7th Marines. On 17 February 1966, the band gave concerts in several key areas for civic action. The band treated the hamlet of Vinh An, where Company A, 1st Battalion, 7th Marines had furnished unusually effective support for revolutionary development, to an impressive performance of western music and precision marching. The band also played at Tri Binh (1) and Nuoc Man and was applauded enthusiastically by the villagers. Two days later, at the Da Nang Catholic cathedral, in an area neatly cordoned off with white nylon line and with Vietnamese and U. S. flags flying, the drum and bugle corps performed before a huge curious crowd. Drum head designs set the theme of the presentation with flags of both states combined with a handshake symbol. The words, "Friendship Through Music," in Vietnamese tied together the theme. The Vietnamese responded ecstatically.(31) From that time onward, both the band and the drum and bugle corps became purposeful weapons in the campaign to place the Vietnamese people behind the government. Marines also began to include music appreciation periods along with English classes in order to appeal to the Vietnamese interested in music and drama.

Operation DOUBLE EAGLE:
the Team of Civic Action and Psychological Warfare
in Support of a Major Operation

By late January 1966, civic action was becoming more closely integrated into large unit operations of the Marine Corps, especially with the successful precedent of Operation MALLARD and various lesser cordon and search operations of 1965. On 28 January 1966, III MAF conducted the largest amphibious operation since the Korean War. The Marines of several battalions landed from shipping of the Amphibious Task Group of the Seventh Fleet near Thach Tru south of Chu Lai. The landing was part of a month-long joint ARVN/U. S. Marine Corps operation called DOUBLE EAGLE.(32) The operation showed the advances in Marine Corps thoughts about the team of civic action and psychological warfare in Vietnam. HQ, III MAF ensured that a civic action organization was included in the Marine Corps task organization. Two U. S. Army Civil Affairs Teams also came under Marine Corps control and were used to handle refugees and to assist the Vietnamese District Chief of Duc Pho (located approximately 50 miles south of Chu Lai on Highway One) in processing and caring for the expected influx of people. The civic action group brought ashore large quantities of basic supplies to support civilians separated from their homes and to care for the expected refugees. The Marine Corps supported Operation DOUBLE EAGLE with more than 27 tons of food specifically for the care of civilians in the operating area. Claims against the Marine Corps for damage to crops, homes, etc., had been a persistent problem in Vietnam also. But the Civic Action Officer for DOUBLE EAGLE carried with him a special fund of 3,665 piasters to deal on the spot with small claims.(33)

The lessons learned about civic action in Operations MALLARD and DOUBLE EAGLE reinforced each other. To be effective, Marine Corps civic action had to be coordinated through the Vietnamese district government. The Marine Corps depended on the district headquarters to collect, classify, and clear all refugees and displaced persons once they had been transported to the general area of the district headquarters by Marine Corps helicopter or truck. The processes carried out by the Vietnamese with the exception of collection, were political and administrative and were a function of local government. The Marine Corps learned that the large quantities of captured foodstuffs and similar materials were best processed through the closest district headquarters. The Vietnamese officials were best equipped by language and local knowledge to effect redistribution. The major civic action lesson of both MALLARD and DOUBLE EAGLE was that coordination between the Marine Corps and local Vietnamese government ensured the greatest and most lasting effect on the local population.(34)

Marines carried out a major psychological warfare effort in support of DOUBLE EAGLE. Propaganda themes directed at the Viet Cong fighter predominated in the written and oral attacks against the enemy. The themes were both short and long-range and were capable of being used against civilians also. The Psychological Section coordinated the dropping of almost three million leaflets in the objective area during the first part of the operation. The Marine Corps received nine ralliers during the first phase of DOUBLE EAGLE largely as a result of emphasizing Viet Cong hardships and making it easy for the enemy to defect. Aerial loudspeaker systems proved especially effective and they broadcast the same effective themes found on the leaflets: Viet Cong lack of food, poor medical care, separation from home and family; as well as the strength of the GVN and its allies, surrender appeals, and explanations of how to surrender.(35)

Medical Assistance Twelve Months after the Landing

During February 1966, III MAF recovered handily from the adverse effects of TET on medical assistance. Units of III MAF using 40 MEDCAP teams treated either medically or dentally almost 67,000 Vietnamese citizens in 122 locations. The most

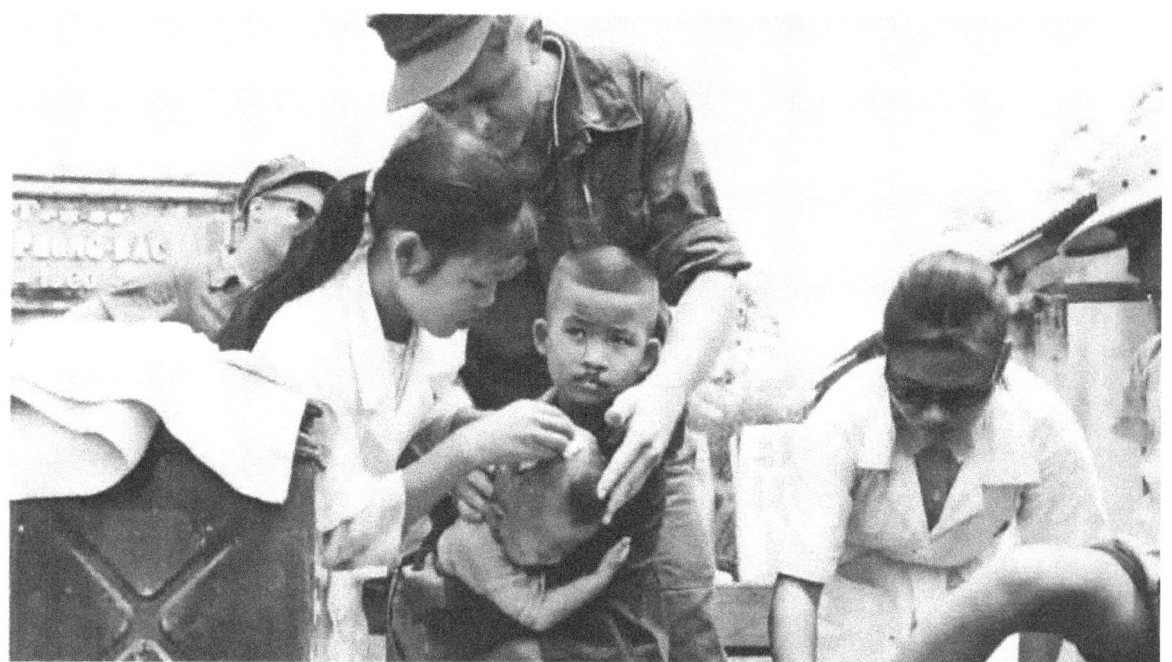

Medical assistance was the mainstay of civic action. The more advanced type is shown in this scene where two girls are being trained as rural health workers. The reinforcement of the Vietnamese rural health program was the goal of Marine assistance. Lt G.L. Williams MC,USN, supervises one of the girls who is treating a case of skin infection. 18Sep65 (USMC A185695)

Medical assistance even at the end of March 1966 was not an elaborate thing. In this photograph taken in March in the Chu Lai TAOR, a corpsman of the 7th Marines begins to treat a moderate-sized gathering consisting largely of children. (USMC A369926)

numerous ailments continued to be skin diseases, headaches, and
respiratory infections which formed well over half of the ailments of individual citizens. In addition to medical treatment,
and probably more important from the long-range viewpoint,
Navy corpsmen trained 16 health workers, two volunteer nurses,
and four volunteer medical assistants. By February, the medical training programs had taken on special importance as a
source of Vietnamese medical personnel. Prior to December
1965, the GVN had insisted on giving the trainees the normal
examination for hiring as health workers. The scheduling,
testing, and correcting process was time consuming and
affected the morale of the trainees. Additionally, the process
did little to further the prestige of the U. S. military force
which had conducted the training. The Vietnamese Minister of
Health decided, therefore, on 4 December 1965, to hire auto-
matically Vietnamese citizens trained by U. S. military/naval
medical teams if the programs were approved in advance. As a
result, by February 1966, appreciable numbers of Vietnamese
medical trainees were flowing through III MAF medical training
programs directly into the Public Health Service.(36)

The Marine Corps Reserve Civic Action Fund for Vietnam
was used by CARE to provide major quantities of food as well
as blacksmith kits, carpenter kits, and more than 2,000 textile
kits. CARE delivered over 37 tons of rice to III MAF and this
rice and the large number of textile kits represented a change
in emphasis from previous months. Formerly, CARE had used the
reserve fund primarily for school supplies. HQ, III MAF ensured that all of the material received during February was
delivered to local government officials who actually distributed the supplies to the Vietnamese people. In the immediate
vicinity of Da Nang, the powerful Buddhist faction of the population controlled an important system of schools and orphanages.
Here, the CG, III MAF, supported the Buddhist program with
large outlays from his reserve civic action contingency fund.
General Walt had contributed over 9,000 dollars (U.S.) in
support by February 1966.(37)

Project HANDCLASP

Project HANDCLASP, an official Navy program since 1962,
shipped 63,000 pounds of miscellaneous, basic commodities to
III MAF in February 1966. HANDCLASP was part of the Navy's
people-to-people effort and overseas community relations
program; and, since 1963, the Navy had been shipping HANDCLASP
materials to Vietnam. Individuals and organizations within
the United States donated material to the naval service and
shipped it to warehouses at San Diego for further delivery by
the Navy overseas. With the buildup of Navy and Marine Corps
forces in Vietnam in 1965, the Navy began to emphasize civic
action programs within Vietnam for both Navy and Marine Corps
forces. Prior to 1965, HANDCLASP had been a Navy program only,

but in June 1965, the Commander in Chief, Pacific Fleet, notified the CG, III MAF that HANDCLASP supplies were available for use by the Marine Corps. The materials which were available were basic and included, clothing, food supplements, medical supplies, and books. The CG, III MAF accepted the support and requested in particular the following items: pens, soap, vitamin and worm pills, sewing needles, thread, and salt. The CG's request reflected in microcosm the whole Marine Corps civic action program. Pens reflected education; soap, and vitamin and worm pills reflected pressing necessities in medical aid; sewing needles and thread represented self-help for clothing; and salt was the most basic of food necessities.(38)

Project HANDCLASP became one of the major sources of supplies for Marine Corps civic action, but the project operated on a tenuous basis. Handclasp was a nonfunded activity of the Navy which meant that the Navy was able to move material only on a space available basis in naval shipping and aircraft. For example, Military Sea Transport Service ships and Military Air Transport Service aircraft could not be used to deliver Handclasp material. As a result, the shipment of material depended on naval operational requirements for space and the flow was uneven. After early 1965 naval operational commitments increased and threatened the effectiveness of the program in the Western Pacific. Simultaneously, however, the Navy realized the importance of civic action in the Vietnamese war and the end result was that space was made available. The shipment of Handclasp supplies rose sharply in 1966. Nevertheless, American charity seemed to be practically limitless and the final check on the program was limitations in shipping space.(39)

The Breadth of Civic Action by March 1966:
From Candy to County Fair

By March 1966, after one year of operations in Vietnam, Marine Corps units were carrying out a broad range of civic action. Contrast, for example, the receipt of private U. S. charity commodities via naval operational shipping for use in soft and indirect civic action, i.e., the distribution of commodities through local governing officials, with the following technique. The 3d Marine Division originally tested something called the County Fair concept on a pilot basis in February 1966. The concept was a variant of Marine Corps cordon and search operations which had been used as early as August 1965 in the Da Nang TAOR by the 9th Marines.(40) The concept was further refined after February and established by March 1966 as a standard type of operation for division units.

County Fair was a joint Marine Corps/ARVN operation designed to destroy Viet Cong influence in chosen hamlets and to reestablish the authority of the GVN. Marine Corps units provided security during the County Fair operations by cordoning off chosen hamlets with riflemen alert for a possible breakout by Viet Cong guerrilla fighters. Surprise was the vital necessity during the positioning of the cordon; if surprise were complete, members of the Viet Cong infrastructure would be trapped within the cordon. ARVN forces and GVN political workers then entered the cordoned area and moved all of the villagers to a central area where they were interrogated, processed for identification, fed, and exposed to propaganda lectures, drama presentations, and movies. While this combined military and civic action was being carried out, ARVN forces conducted a detailed search of the hamlet for hidden tunnels, food, munitions, and hiding Viet Cong.(41)

County Fair was designed to destroy the laboriously established Viet Cong infrastructure within a hamlet or village by trapping the Viet Cong within the inhabited complex and then methodically using police and intelligence techniques to isolate the Viet Cong from the villagers. Well conducted County Fair operations impressed the villagers with the power, efficiency, and benevolence of the GVN.(42) The operations in their refined form were a traumatic surprise to the Viet Cong, who emphasized in captured documents the necessity to take immediate countermeasures against the new technique. The Viet Cong concentrated on two defenses against County Fair: first, if surprise were not complete, every effort had to be bent towards breaking through the incomplete cordon; second, acknowledging that surprise might be complete, the Viet Cong ordered the preparation of stocks of food and water to support passive hiding for periods of three to five days.(43)

County Fair operations emphasized Marine Corps support for hard civic action, i.e., security and direct support for Vietnamese revolutionary development. They were a far cry from the candy and pill patrols of April 1965. They were also different from the distribution of Handclasp commodities in secure areas in March 1966. County Fair operations and Combined Action Companies represented Marine Corps civic action in its hardest and most aggressive state by March. Both concepts had been proven successful by the anniversary of the first year of major Marine Corps forces in Vietnam. In February 1966, the first CAC had been formed in the Da Nang TAOR in emulation of the successful company at Hue/Phu Bai. And shortly thereafter, III MAF introduced the CAC concept at Chu Lai. County Fair operations began to expand rapidly also. In March 1966, III MAF conducted a total of four County Fair operations under the immediate direction of HQ, 9th Marines. Several months later, in July 1966, operations numbered in the twenties and were taking place in all of the TAORs.(44)

The Importance of Civic Action:
Indicators of Progress

At the end of the first year in Vietnam, Marine Corps civic action with its many ramifications had become so important that it ranked almost equally with the formal combat effort. General Walt specifically emphasized the operational concept of two powerful hands, one a clenched fist used to smash the enemy main force and guerrilla fighters, and the other open and extended to the Vietnamese people to shield them from the terror and to assist their government. But HQ, III MAF found it difficult to describe or present civic action progress. Combat actions were measurable in terms of the numbers of actions fought, patrols run, and ambushes laid as well as the number of casualties inflicted on the enemy. But HQ, III MAF for the first year had no satisfactory system of quantifying the results of civic action in support of revolutionary development. Assuredly, HQ, III MAF had collected statistics on civic action including number of medical treatments, number of persons treated (uniformly a lower figure), pounds of food and clothing distributed, etc.. But the statistics were not satisfactorily correlated with progress in the war until February 1966.

Progress in the war largely depended on the advancement of Vietnamese revolutionary development. In February 1966, in an attempt to relate civic action to that progress, HQ, III MAF adopted a system of rating the progress of Vietnamese revolutionary development in the Marine Corps TAORs in ICTZ. The system was important because it not only related civic action and revolutionary development but also tied in Marine Corps combat operations with the latter. For the first time the Marine Corps had a system which allowed it to estimate its general progress in the Vietnamese struggle. The system essentially equated progress in revolutionary development to progress in the war in general and included certain indicators of progress which could only be accomplished by the Marine Corps or a similar military organization, e.g., ARVN. The system included the following general indicators of progress:*

1. Destruction of enemy units------------20 Points
2. Destruction of enemy infrastructure---20 Points
3. GVN establishment of security--------20 Points
4. GVN establishment of local government-20 Points
5. Degree of development, new
    life program-------------------------20 Points
                Total----------------100 Points

(Equivalent to accomplishment of revolutionary development)(45)

* See Chart Number Two for a detailed breakdown of these indicators.

Chart Number Two

Detailed Breakdown of the Revolutionary Development
Indicators of Progress

			POINTS
1.	Destruction of Enemy Units		
	a. VC units destroyed or expelled		15
	b. Local defensive force established		5
		TOTAL	20
2.	Destruction of Enemy Infrastructure		
	a. Village census completed		2
	b. VC infrastructure destroyed		8
	c. Local intelligence net established		5
	d. Census, grievance interviews completed		2
	e. Action completed on grievances		3
		TOTAL	20
3.	Vietnamese Establishment of Security		
	a. Defensive plan completed		2
	b. Defensive installations completed		3
	c. Security forces trained and in place		12
	d. Communications net established		3
		TOTAL	20
4.	Establishment of Local Governments		
	a. Village chief and council in office		4
	b. Village chief residing in village		3
	c. Hamlet chiefs and councils in office		4
	d. Hamlet chiefs residing in hamlet		4
	e. Psychological operations and information program established		3
	f. Minimum social and administrative organization		2
		TOTAL	20
5.	Degree of New Life Program Development		
	a. Adequate public health program		4
	b. Adequate education facilities		4
	c. Adequate agricultural development		4
	d. Adequate transportation facilities		4
	e. Necessary markets established		4
		TOTAL	20

III MAF had the mission within its TAOR of destroying the main force of the Viet Cong and the guerrilla forces. This combat mission was closely linked with Vietnamese revolutionary development because the indispensable factor for the beginning of RD in the Marine Corps TAORs was successful combat against the overt fighting elements of the Viet Cong. But III MAF, with remarkable candidness, rated the destruction or expulsion of Viet Cong combat units at only 15 percent of the accomplishment of RD. The Marine Corps combat effort provided the shield behind which the complex, political, economic, social, and paramilitary action could take place which formed the remaining 85 percent of revolutionary development.(46)

Marine Corps civic action meshed with revolutionary development in a broader range of the RD indicators than combat operations. For example, 25 percent of the "destruction of enemy units" involved the establishment of a local defense force. By February 1966, HQ, III MAF had established two Combined Action Companies and had conducted systematic training for large numbers of Popular Forces, thus making an important contribution to RD by means of the hard or security type of civic action. Eighty-five percent of the "Vietnamese establishment of security" comprised the training of Popular Forces, planning for defense, and the construction of defensive installations. Again, Marine Corps civic action directly supported adequate public health programs, education facilities, transportation facilities, agricultural development, and the establishment of markets. Considering the support of public health programs alone in March 1966, III MAF gave medical treatment to more than 84,000 Vietnamese citizens and was in the process of training 77 persons as medical assistants of various types. The RD indicators placed the medical effort of III MAF in a meaningful relationship with the general progress of the war. The establishment of an adequate public health program was rated at only four percent of the total accomplishment of revolutionary development.(47)

Principles of Effective Civic Action for Vietnam

By March 1966, the Marine Corps had formulated effective principles of civic action. The Marine Corps had advanced beyond its initial defensive military mission and had become part of a full-blooded effort to establish a viable South Vietnamese government. The broader outlook of the Marine Corps in its new role in revolutionary war was strongly etched in the new principles which included purposeful support for local government at the expense, if necessary, of the acknowledgement of Marine Corps assistance. The Marine Corps had faced revolutionary movements in the past in the Central American and the Caribbean areas. But the disciplined insurgent organization in Vietnam and the international complications rendered the Vietnamese situation so much more intense that it had to be ranked as something different in Marine Corps experience.(48)

The principles of effective civic action for Vietnam comprised more than a dry-as-dust list of etiquette for relations between Marines and officials and citizens of the Republic of Vietnam. The principles represented a new form of warfare, a concept balanced between sophisticated modern combat and direct support for indigenous political, social, and economic action. Six points could be differentiated; together they formed a pronouncement of the Marine Corps response to "the struggle to rescue the people"(49) from a subtle, intellectually brilliant form of warfare.

First, Marine Corps civic action programs had to be continuous. Discontinuity and incompletion were synonymous with failure. Civic action programs were responsible acts which were promises of benefits to a seriously demoralized population. Failure to produce the promised benefits allowed the irresponsible Viet Cong to outbid the government in power by promising superior results at an undefined future time. Ultimately, no Marine Corps civic action could be lasting unless it were part of a program requested and needed by the local Vietnamese population and allocated the resources required for completion and continuation by the national government. To provide real continuity the Marine Corps had to support Vietnamese projects rather than, with misplaced zeal, create Marine Corps projects.

Second, civic action had to function through local Vietnamese officials. Again, the tendency to produce Marine Corps programs or to work through individuals had to be strictly controlled.(50) Only Vietnamese programs could be tolerated and support of those programs had to take place through Vietnamese governing officials. However, spontaneous humanitarian acts and contacts between individual Marines and Vietnamese citizens were exceptions to functioning within the Vietnamese chain of governmental command. These acts and contacts were important adjuncts to the Vietnamese programs encompassing revolutionary development and the programs of rural health, agricultural assistance, etc.. The spontaneous Marine Corps acts served to popularize the Marine Corps and the government which it had come to support. But Marine Corps civic action was not a popularity contest between Marines and the local population. Even though the spontaneous acts and individual contacts were important, they had to fit within the framework of a disciplined, single-minded program of support for the Vietnamese government. An enemy so ruthless and well-entrenched as the Vietnamese communist of the mid-1960s could be successfully overcome only by the discipline, purpose, and control possible within a first-class military organization.(51)

Third, civic action programs had to be related to the basic needs of the rural population. The production of food was the central issue of life for most of the Vietnamese people. Concentration of effort, one of the principles of war and a

Support for education: a winsome young orphan at Trung Phu Orphanage south of Da Nang receives booklets from a Marine visitor early in 1966. By this time support for education had become a vital part of civic action. The Marine Corps Reserve Civic Action Fund which had been announced in Sep 65 concentrated initially on the buying of CARE school kits. (MCA187646)

Support for the rural school system: in a well organized program at Le Tinh village near Chu Lai, LtCol Paul X. Kelley, CO, 2nd Battalion, 4th Marines presents precious school supplies to a child. Note the schoolmaster (raised hands) prompting the children, ARVN soldier (beret), loudspeaker system (upper right), and the Vietnamese flag. (USMC A369053)

sound principle of business management, ruled the field in the case of basic needs. Marine Corps civic action had neither the resources nor the time to support frivolous activities. The Viet Cong and predecessor Viet Minh had operated in parts of the South Vietnamese countryside for a quarter of a century. In the I Corps Tactical Zone, the Viet Cong had made important advances in 1964 and these were characterized by meticulous attention to honesty in dealings with farmers and fishermen. In both its earlier operations and the more recent ones, the Viet Cong had displayed a masterful grasp of what was real to the peasant and the fisherman. The Marine Corps had to reveal to the rural population the same benevolent realism. But the pressing, basic needs of the countryside could be most effectively determined by the people themselves. And even though the Marine Corps could determine by pure reason that support for food production was the basic need of the people, the precise programs for implementation were so complex as to require playing the subtle game of waiting for the request of the local peasant for assistance.(52)

Fourth, once civic action programs had begun which were requested by the people, were coordinated with Vietnamese revolutionary development, and had been assured of the resources necessary for completion and continuation, the Marine Corps had to bend every effort to enhance the prestige of the local officials who were directing the programs. The assassination of effective governing officials was one of the mainstays of Viet Cong political action. Marine Corps civic action projects had to enhance the reputation of Vietnamese officials who were able to produce concrete gains for the peasants and provide justice. Support and protection for honest officials was the foundation for Marine Corps civic action. Even the Southeast Asian form of the Marxist dialectic would find it a tortuous path to justify assassination of effective and honest men. Marine Corps civic action had to help to create those men and support their actions. Marine Corps rifles would make the Viet Cong form of public "execution" a greater challenge than the cheap exercise in deliberate terror which it had been in the past.

Fifth, in the cases where choices existed, Marines had to choose civic action projects with the shortest time of completion. The mobility of the Marine Corps and its preoccupation with combat against the main forces and the guerrillas of the Viet Cong movement emphasized the reality that long-term projects and ultimately revolutionary development were the responsibility of the people and the Government of Vietnam. Assuredly, the Marine Corps would support both individual long-term projects and revolutionary development; but Marine Corps support was forced to take the form of short-term projects within the framework of the larger, longer ones. For example, medical assistance was one of the keystones of Marine Corps civic action and was probably the essence of short-term, high-impact civic action. But the most effective medical assistance was that which reinforced the existing Vietnamese rural health service and that carried out as part of revolutionary development. It was generally true that the words, short-term and high-impact, best described Marine Corps civic action. But the levels of service established in programs involving Marine Corps support had to be delicately curtailed in many cases to ensure the same level of service after the departure of the Marine units.

Sixth, civic action encouraged and supported projects which used Vietnamese talent and materials to the maximum practical extent. A guiding principle in civic action projects proved to be self-help on the part of the peasantry. Self-help projects meant more to the peasants than gifts; and the Viet Cong, who were barometers of the effectiveness of Marine Corps actions, normally avoided damage to projects which were the result of peasant labor. On the other hand, government or Marine Corps projects were fair game for criticism and destruction. The peasants had to have a predominating influence in projects which were, after all, aimed at beneficial change for them. Marine Corps ingenuity could never be allowed to predominate if civic action programs were going to have lasting significance for the Vietnamese people and be a source of lasting influence for their governing officials.(53)

Clothes for old women: clothes along with food and medicine were the most important commodities distributed by Marines. The essence of this view seems to be that happiness is a bundle of old clothes. The youngster looks pleased also. The distribution was made late in 1966 at Ly Son island off the coast near Chu Lai by MAG-26. (USMC A421460)

NOTES

Chapter I

1. Based on 1stLt Kenneth W. Clem, Ltr. <u>Background Data on Killed or Captured Viet Cong</u>, dtd 17 April 1967, presently on file in Historical Branch, G-3 Division, HQ, U. S. Marine Corps.

2. Clem, Ltr., <u>Background Data</u>, 17Apr67.

3. Vietnamese villages often include hamlets with identical names differentiated only by a following numeral.

4. <u>New York Times</u>, 8 March 1965, p. A-3.

5. Commanding Officer, 2d Battalion, 3d Marines, <u>Ltr 6/DAC/kl, 5700 16 June 1965</u> to Commanding General, III MAF, paras 1-4.

6. William A. Nighswonger, <u>Rural Pacification in Vietnam: 1962-1965</u> (Advanced Research Projects Agency, Office of the Secretary of Defense; May 1966), pp. 138-154. See also HQ (G-2), FMFPac, <u>A Marine's Guide to the Republic of Vietnam</u>, 11 May 1966.

7. FMFPac, <u>III MAF Operations</u>, December 1966 (S), pp. 30, 31.

8. 2d Battalion, 1st Marines, <u>Command Chronology, February 1966</u> (S). The 2d Battalion, 1st Marines was the successor to the 3d Battalion, 4th Marines at Hue/Phu Bai and continued the CAC operations of the former unit.

Chapter II

1. U. S. Department of State, Bureau of Public Affairs, Office of Media Services, <u>Vietnam Information Notes</u>, Number 1, February 1967, pp. 2, 3.

2. Bernard B. Fall, <u>The Two Viet-Nams: A Political and Military Analysis</u>, Revised Edition (New York: 1965), pp. 252-253. 336.

3. See the <u>New York Times</u>, 13 June 1965, for a concise summary of the political shifts in Vietnam from November 1963-June 1965.

4. <u>Washington Post</u>, 19 June 1965, p. 1. See also Ky's description of the critical nature of the Vietnamese situation in the <u>Washington Post</u>, 20 June 1965, p. 1.

5. "Charts" and "Summaries" provided by Mr. J. J. Helble, Office of South Vietnamese Affairs, Department of State, dtd 1 March 1965, 19 June 1965, 12 October 1965, 21 February 1966, 13 July 1966, 18 November 1966, and 28 January 1967 (hereinafter referred to as Helble, "Charts" and "Summaries").

6. Single Sheet entitled The Government of the Republic of Vietnam, Field Administration and Local Government, Unofficial as of January 1966, and Produced by the U. S. Agency for International Development, Public Administration Division. See also, Department of State, Agency for International Development, A Vietnamese District Chief in Action, pp. 19, 31. The term, hamlet, is used in this paper to include the traditional "thon" or small village (hamlet) and the "xa" or village of normal size. The term, village, is used to refer to the grouped village or unit of administrative convenience.

7. Headquarters, U. S. Marine Corps, G-3 Division, Civic Action Branch, Notes for Public Appearances (effective March 1967), p. 2. The quotation has a certain poetical meter and was quoted in its most effective form.

8. George A. Carver, Jr. "The Faceless Viet Cong," Foreign Affairs, Vol. 44, No. 3, April 1966, pp. 347-372. Carver's work is a detailed analysis of the organization of the Viet Cong movement. Carver emphasizes the use of terror by the Viet Cong and notes that the main strength of the movement is in the countryside.

9. Chief of Staff, U. S. Army, Deputy Chief of Staff for Military Operations, Civil Affairs, Plans and Policies Division, Civic Action Branch, Revolutionary Development Planning, p. 2.

10. Headquarters, U. S. Military Assistance Command, Vietnam, MACJ332, dtd 23 November 1965, Establishment of the 1966 Rural Construction (Pacification) Plan, pp. 1, 2.

11. Helble, "Charts" and "Summaries".

12. Richard C. Kriegel, Jr., Revolutionary Development: Last Chance for Victory in Vietnam, pp. 1-12. This document is a pamphlet presently on file in the Historical Branch, G-3 Division, HQ, U. S. Marine Corps. Kriegel was one of the U. S. advisors to General Thang at the National Training Center, Vung Tau, in 1966. General Thang carried out the training of the revolutionary development cadres at Vung Tau.

Chapter III

1. Jerome of Westphalia originated the remark that "man could do anything with bayonets but sit on them." He made the remark during a conversation with his redoubtable relative, Napoleon I.

2. Headquarters, Department of the Army, <u>Civil Affairs Operations</u>, Field Manual No. 41-10, p. 88.

3. <u>Ibid</u>.

4. In 1965 the government's plan to secure the countryside, and hence, the state was called rural construction. The term revolutionary development appeared at the turn of 1966 and replaced the words, rural construction, as the general description of the government's plan for survival.

5. Chief of Staff, U. S. Army, Deputy Chief of Staff for Military Operations, Civil Affairs, Civic Action Branch, <u>Revolutionary Development Planning</u>, pp. 1-4.

6. HQ, U. S. Marine Corps, G-3 Division, Civic Action Branch, <u>Notes for Public Appearances</u>, p. 5. The definition was a general one. A definition applying more directly to the situation in Vietnam was found in <u>III MAF Order 1750.1, 7 June 1965</u>, p. 1.

7. <u>Ibid</u>., p. 4. The definition was based on, Departments of the Army, Navy, and the Air Force, <u>Joint Manual for Civil Affairs, November 1966</u>, para. 4-5.

8. Nighswonger, <u>Rural Pacification</u>, pp. 161-166.

9. Chief of Staff, U. S. Army, Deputy Chief of Staff for Military Operations, Civil Affairs, Civic Action Branch, <u>Chart: US/GVN Organization for Revolutionary Development, SVN</u>.

10. Nighswonger, <u>Rural Pacification</u>, p. 287. The author emphasizes the central importance of security for any progress in revolutionary development.

11. Major Charles J. Keever, <u>III MAF Civic Action Summary</u>, pp. 7-13. This document is a 16-page authoritative description of Marine Corps civic action by the first Civic Action Officer of III MAF.

Chapter IV

1. HQ, U. S. Marine Corps, G-3 Division, Historical Branch, Manuscript, *Marine Corps Operations in Vietnam, January 1965-June 1965* (S) p. 8.

2. U. S. Department of State, White Paper, "Aggression from the North," excerpts in *The Viet-Nam Reader: Articles and documents on American Foreign Policy in the Viet-Nam Crisis*, ed. by Marcus G. Raskin and Bernard B. Fall (New York: 1965), pp. 143-154.

3. *Washington Post*, 8 March 1965, p. 1. See also the *Philadelphia Inquirer*, 8 March 1965, p. 1 and the editorial page.

4. 9th MEB, *Command Chronology*, March 1965 (S), pp. 1, 2.

5. Fleet Marine Force, Pacific, Operations of the *III Marine Amphibious Force, Vietnam, March-September 1965* (S), pp. 1, 5, 18.

6. 9th MEB, *Command Chronology, March 1965* (S). The whole chronology exudes concern over the problems of the buildup.

7. 9th MEB, *Command Chronology, April 1965* (S), p. 4.

8. FMFPac, *Operations of the III Marine Amphibious Force, Vietnam, March-September 1965* (S), pp. 17-24.

9. *Washington Post*, 7 May 1965.

10. 3d MAB *Command Diary*, April/May 1965, p. 23.

11. LtCol David A. Clement, *Taped Interview #189: Civic Action Program of the 2d Battalion, 3d Marines*, pp. 63-77.

12. FMFPac, *III MAF Operations, March-September 1965*, (S), pp. 26-31.

13. HQ, USMACV, Letter of Instruction, *Da Nang Administrative Coordination*, 29 May 1965, pp. 1-3.

14. Force Order 1750.1, *Concepts of Civic Action in the Republic of Vietnam*, 7 June 1965.

15. *Ibid.*, p. 1. The problems were described succinctly under the heading, "Background."

16. *Ibid.*, p. 2, para. 2.

17. *Ibid.*, p. 2, para. 6.

18. See the Howard Margolis column in The Washington Post, 11 June 1965.

19. HQ, III MAF, Civic Action Report, 8 March-15 July 1965, dtd 18 July 1965, Enclosures (4), (5), (6), (10), (13), (14), (16).

20. Ibid., Enclosure (13).

21. 3d Battalion, 4th Marines, Command Chronology, June 1965 (S), pp. 1-3 of the Narrative.

22. FMFPac, III MAF Operations, March-September 1965, (S), pp. 27, 35. The exact figures were 8,204 (25May65) and 17,601 (15Jun65).

23. HQ, III MAF, Civic Action Report, 8 March-15 July 1965, Enclosure (13).

24. Ibid.

25. 1stLt William F. B. Francis, Taped Interview #120: Work as Civil Affairs Officer, 3d Marines, 15 April-15 July 1965, pp. 38-51.

26. Ibid., p. 49.

27. Ibid., p. 40.

28. Ibid., pp. 50, 51.

29. Capt Lionel V. Silva, Taped Interview #37: Civic Action in the Le My Area, pp. 1-18.

30. Ibid., pp. 6-7.

31. See the remarkably detailed account of the action in the Baltimore Sun, 1 July 1965, p. 1. See also, HQ, U. S. Marine Corps, Division of Information, United Press International Clips, 1600 (local time) 1 July 1965.

32. FMFPac, III MAF Operations, March-September 1965 (S) pp. 33, 34.

33. III MAF, Command Chronology, July 1965 (S), p. 6.

34. III MAF Order 5800.3, 17 June 1965, Civic Action Medical Teams, p. 3.

35. III MAF, Command Chronology, July 1965 (S), p. 6.

36. HQ, III MAF, Civic Action Reports, 8 March-15 July 1965, p. 2.

37. *Ibid.*, Enclosure (3), p. 2.

38. <u>CARE</u> <u>Fact</u> <u>Sheet</u>, effective May 1967, pp. 1, 3.

39. See <u>OPNAV</u> <u>Instruction</u> <u>5726.3A</u>, dtd 28 August 1964, and the information sheet, Commander J. F. Dow, <u>Project</u> <u>Handclasp</u>/<u>Civic</u> <u>Action</u>, dtd 10 November 1965.

40. 3d Engineer Battalion (Reinf) (Forward), <u>Command</u> <u>Chronology</u>, <u>1-31</u> <u>July</u> <u>1965</u> (S), Part II, third and fourth pages (pages not numbered).

41. The problem of payment of claims was especially important in both the Da Nang and Chu Lai TAORs because of the problems of airfield construction, maintenance, and defense.

42. Keever, <u>III</u> <u>MAF</u> <u>Civic</u> <u>Action</u> <u>Summary</u>, pp. 3-4.

43. HQ, 4th Marines, <u>Regimental</u> <u>Order</u> <u>6000.1</u>, dtd 23 June 1965, pp. 1-2.

44. HQ, III MAF, <u>Civic</u> <u>Action</u> <u>Report</u>, <u>8</u> <u>March</u>-<u>15</u> <u>July</u> <u>1965</u>, Encl. (14).

45. In 1965 and 1966 civilian personnel of the U. S. Operations Mission were established no lower than province level. The situation was only beginning to change by April 1967. See the chart entitled, <u>US</u>/<u>GVN</u> <u>Organization</u> <u>for</u> <u>Revolutionary</u> <u>Development</u> and held by U. S. Army, Office of the Chief of Operations, Civil Affairs Division, Civic Action Branch.

46. III MAF, <u>Combat</u> <u>Information</u> <u>Bureau</u>, <u>Release</u> <u>No</u>. <u>247-65</u>, 16 July 1965. See also <u>Pacific</u> <u>Stars</u> <u>and</u> <u>Stripes</u>, 26 July 1965.

47. CO, 2d Battalion, 3d Marines, Ltr 6/DAC/klj, 5700, 16Jun65, Reconstruction of <u>Le</u> <u>My</u> (known to local people as Hoa Loc village, district of Hoa Vang, province of Quang Nam), Encl: (9).

48. 1st Battalion, 3d Marines, <u>Command</u> <u>Chronology</u>, <u>July</u> <u>1965</u> (S), Situation Report 104, 19 July 1965.

49. See, for example, Commanding Officer, 2d Battalion, 3d Marines, <u>Ltr</u> <u>6/DAC/kl</u>, <u>5700</u> <u>16</u> <u>June</u> <u>1965</u>, para. 3.

50. Special Operations Research Office, American University, <u>Human</u> <u>Factors</u> <u>Considerations</u> <u>of</u> <u>Undergrounds</u> <u>in</u> <u>Insurgencies</u>, 1 December 1965, pp. 182, 183. This document appeared in September 1966 as Department of the Army Pamphlet No. 550-104.

51. FMFPac, <u>III</u> <u>MAF</u> <u>Operations</u>, <u>March</u>-<u>September</u> <u>1965</u> (S), pp. 11-14. See also, 3d Battalion, 9th Marines, <u>Civic</u> <u>Action</u> <u>Situation</u> <u>Report</u>, <u>2</u> <u>December</u> <u>1965</u>.

Chapter V

1. Interview with Col Don P. Wyckoff, dtd 5 June 1967. Col Wyckoff was the Assistant Chief of Staff, G-3, 3d MarDiv in August 1965.

2. Keever, III MAF Civic Action Summary, pp. 6-8, 10.

3. See the description of the various civic action programs in HQ, III MAF, Civic Action Report, 8 March-15 July 1965, Enclosures (1), (2), (3), for a brief, general description of civic action through the middle of July.

4. HQ, III MAF, Minutes of Planning Meeting /for a Regional Working Group/, 30 August 1965.

5. HQ, III MAF, Civil Affairs Officer, Memo to Deputy Chief of Staff, 29 August 1965. This document contained a suggested mission which was accepted by the planning meeting of the I Corps JCC on 30 August 1965.

6. HQ, U. S. Marine Corps, G-3 Division, Civic Action Branch, I Corps Joint Coordinating Council, Summary of Activities During CY 1966.

7. HQ, III MAF, Minutes of the Meeting of the I Corps Joint Coordinating Council, Statement of Mission, Composition, and Functions I Corps Joint Coordinating Council.

8. HQ, III MAF, Minutes of the Meeting of the I Corps Joint Coordinating Council, 15 November 1965, para. 3.

9. LtCol Verle E. Ludwig, "Bus to Tra Khe," Marine Corps Gazette, vol. 50, no. 10, October 1966, p. 34.

10. Col Bryce F. Denno USA, "Viet Cong Defeat at Phuoc Chau," Marine Corps Gazette, Vol. 49, No. 3, March 1965, p. 35.

11. Recall the quotation of the village elder from, Notes for Public Appearances, Civic Action Branch, G-3 Division, HQ, U. S. Marine Corps: "...the Viet Cong never take anything, they tax...."

12. New York Times, 20 August 1965.

13. Nighswonger, Rural Pacification, pp. 177-179.

14. MSgt George Wilson, "Combined Action," Marine Corps Gazette, Vol. 50, No. 10, October 1966, pp. 28-31.

15. See the article in the Washington Post, 22 September 1965, entitled "Viet Militiamen are Attached to U. S. Marines," by Mr. Jack Foisie, reporter for the Los Angeles Times.

16. Captain Francis J. West, Jr., The CAC as a Catalyst, mimeographed sheet recounting the impressions of Captain West after duty with the CACs in Vietnam in late 1966.

17. HQ, U. S. Marine Corps, Division of Reserve, Mimeographed Sheets Entitled, Marine Corps Civic Action Fund for Vietnam-Summary, two pages.

18. Ronwyn M. Ingraham, Assistant Director, Washington, D. C. Office CARE, Inc., Letter addressed to Major Stevens and Captain Smith, dated 26 August 1965.

19. Marine Corps Order 5710.4, dtd 13 September 1965.

20. HQ, U. S. Marine Corps, Division of Reserve, Reserve Civic Action Fund-Summary, two pages.

Chapter VI

1. See The New York Times, 8 September 1965, p. 1, and The Washington Post, 9 September 1965, p. 12, for details about PIRANHA.

2. Washington News, 7 September 1965, p. 8.

3. FMFPac, III MAF Operations, October 1965 (S), p. 24. See also, FMFPac, III MAF Operations, December 1965 (S), p. 51.

4. FMFPac, III MAF Operations, October 1965 (S), p.23, and FMFPac, III MAF Operations, December 1965 (S), p. 50.

5. III MAF, Command Chronology, October 1965 (S), Part Three, p. 10.

6. HQ, III MAF, Press Release, 29 October 1965.

7. Interview with Capt Thomas J. McGowan, USMC, on 19 April 1967 at HQ, U. S. Marine Corps. Capt McGowan was Executive Officer, Company I, 3d Battalion, 9th Marines at the time of the action.

8. 3d Battalion, 9th Marines, Command Chronology, October 1965 (S), p. 12.

9. 3d Battalion, 9th Marines, Command Chronology, October 1965 (S), p. 10.

10. This rural construction effort had several names including the following: (1) Quang Nam Pacification Project, (2) Ngu Hanh Son (FIVE MOUNTAINS) Pacification Campaign.

11. Nighswonger, Rural Pacification, pp. 150-154. This account is thin on detail but does emphasize the importance of security

and the challenge of rural construction after two years of
Viet Cong gains.

12. 3d Battalion, 3d Marines, *Civic Action Situation Reports*,
Reports Nos. 1-7, Operation FIVE MOUNTAINS.

13. 3d Battalion, 3d Marines, *Civic Action Situation Report*,
3 January 1966, Report No. 7, Operation FIVE MOUNTAINS.

14. FMFPac, *III MAF Operations, November 1965* (S), p. 16.

15. FMFPac, *III MAF Operations, November 1965* (S), p. 2.

16. A small unit was defined as a company or smaller organization.

17. Clem, Ltr, *Background Data*, 17 April 1967.

18. Nighswonger, *Rural Pacification*, pp. 95, 285-288, 291-292.
See also, 3d Battalion, 3d Marines, *Civic Action Situation
Report, 21 December 1965*, Report No. 6, Operation FIVE MOUNTAINS.

19. 1st Battalion, 3d Marines, *Civic Action Situation Report
15 December 1965*. The Report shows the medical activity of
the battalion on 13 December 1965 and gives a lucid picture of
the effectiveness of the mobile concept. A total of 655 persons
were assisted on 13 December 1965.

20. 3d Battalion, 9th Marines, *Command Chronology, November
1965* (S), p. 7.

21. Ibid., p. 8.

22. 3d Battalion, 9th Marines, *Command Chronology, November
1965* (S), Enclosure (8), After Action Report No. 8-65.

23. *Ibid*.

24. *Ibid*., p. 9.

25. 3d Battalion, 9th Marines, *Civic Action Situation Report,
2 December 1965*. The report of 2 December 1965 included part
of the civic action summary for November 1965.

26. FMFPac, *III MAF Operations, December 1965* (S), pp. 50-51.
FMFPac, *III MAF Operations, October 1965* (S), pp. 23-24.
FMFPac, *III MAF Operations, March-September 1965* (S), pp. 32,48.

27. *Ibid*. (The material in this paragraph is based on the
data in the listing preceding it in the text).

28. See the material contained in 3d Marine Division, *Civic Action Situation Reports*, 1-31 December 1965. The information in this massive source supports a view that Marine Corps civic action was not yet fully coordinated with either Vietnamese local government or rural construction.

29. Compare, LtCol Clement, *Taped Interview #189*, pp. 67-69, with 3d Battalion, 7th Marines, *Civic Action Situation Report, 1 January 1966*, to see the unchanged problem of security between June 1965-December 1965.

30. See 3d Marine Division, *Civic Action Situation Reports*, for the months of December and January 1965/1966. They form a voluminous account largely of the soft type of civic action.

31. 3d Battalion, 7th Marines, *Civic Action Situation Report* /hereinafter abbreviated to SitReps/, 1 January 1966.

32. The shot in the back of Mr. Truong's head was probably fired from close range by unhurried gunmen who had downed the chief with three previous shots.

33. See the brief analysis of security in, 3d Battalion, 3d Marines, *Civic Action Situation Report, 21 December 1965*, Report No. 6, Operation FIVE MOUNTAINS.

34. Nighswonger, *Rural Pacification*, pp. 161-163.

35. 3d Battalion, 3d Marines, *Civic Action Sit Rep, 1-7 January 1966, Report Number 7*, Operation **FIVE** MOUNTAINS.

36. *Ibid*.

37. The Republic of Vietnam, Quang Nam Province, Hoa Vang District, the Northwest Zone, *Impressions of the People of Northwest Hoa Vang District, 12 June 1965*. This letter was also included as Enclosure (1) to HQ, III MAF, Ltr. 1/drw 5720 29 June 1965.

38. 3d Battalion, 4th Marines, *Civic Action Sit Rep, 1700, 22 December 1965*. The italics were included in the report.

39. 3d Marine Division, *Civic Action Sit Reps*, 1-7 December 1965. For the quotation see 3d Tank Battalion, *Civic Action Sit Rep, 2 December 1965*.

40. 3d Tank Battalion, *Civic Action Sit Rep*, 25 January 1966.

41. 1st Battalion, 4th Marines, *Civic Action Sit Rep*, 2 January 1966.

42. 1st Amphibian Tractor Battalion, *Civic Action Sit Rep* 25 December 1965.

43. *Ibid.*

Chapter VII

1. 3d Battalion, 3d Marines, *Civic Action Sit Rep*, *3 January 1966*, Report No. 7, Operation FIVE MOUNTAINS.

2. Chief of Staff, U. S. Army, Deputy Chief of Staff for Military Operations, Civil Affairs, Plans and Policies Division, Civic Action Branch, *Revolutionary Development Planning*, pp. 1-4.

3. 3d Marine Division, *Command Chronology*, *January 1966*, p. 22.

4. 3d Battalion, 7th Marines, *Civic Action Sit Rep*, *25 January 1966* After Action Report Operation MALLARD.

5. *Ibid.*

6. *Ibid.*

7. I Corps Joint Coordinating Council, Weekly Meetings, *Minutes*, *27 January 1966*, p. 1.

8. I Corps Joint Coordinating Council, Weekly Meetings, *Minutes*, *22 February 1966*, p. 1.

9. Based on 3d Marine Division, *Civic Action Sit Reps*, 1 December 1965-31 January 1966.

10. Nighswonger, *Rural Pacification*, p. 207.

11. *Ibid.*, p. 208.

12. By the turn of 1966, it was more accurate to speak of Vietnamese plans for change in the countryside as revolutionary development rather than the older term, rural construction.

13. III MAF, *Command Chronology*, *January 1966* (S), p. 14.

14. See FMFPac, *Professional Knowledge Gained from Operational Experience in Vietnam*, *October 1966*, pp. 57-58.

15. *Ibid.*

16. FMFPac, *III MAF Operations*, *January 1966* (S), p. 2.

17. III MAF, *Command Chronology*, *January 1966* (S), p. 14.

18. Definition of a child: a human younger than 18 years of age.

19. 3d Marine Division, <u>Command Chronology, January 1966</u> (S), p. 2, and 1st Marine Air Wing, <u>Command Chronology, January 1966</u> (Unclassified), pp. 3, 4.

20. III MAF, <u>Command Chronology, January 1966</u> (S), p. 14.

21. 1st Battalion, 7th Marines, <u>Civic Action Sit Rep, 10 January 1966</u>, Special Civil Affairs Program of Company A, 1-9 January 1966.

22. Commanding Officer, 2d Battalion, 3d Marines, <u>Ltr 6/DAC/kl, 5700 16 June 1965</u>, para. 4. The letter was addressed to CG, III MAF.

23. 3d Marine Division, Civic Action Situation Reports, 22-31 January 1965.

24. 3d Battalion, 7th Marines, <u>Civic Action Sit Rep, 22 January 1966</u>.

25. 3d Battalion, 7th Marines, <u>Civic Action Sit Reps, 22-23 January 1966</u>.

26. 1st Battalion, 7th Marines, <u>Civic Action Sit Rep, 24 January 1966</u>.

27. 2d Battalion, 9th Marines, <u>Civic Action Sit Rep, 22 January 1966</u>.

28. 2d Battalion, 1st Marines, <u>Civic Action Sit Rep, 21 January 1966</u>.

29. The civic action data presented on the maps was taken from the following source: 3d Marine Division, <u>Civic Action Sit Reps, 13-17 December 1966</u>. Hence, the data represented the civic action of the most numerous part of III MAF and the part which carried out the majority of civic action projects between May 1965-March 1966.

30. 3d Engineer Battalion, <u>Civic Action Sit Rep, 12 January 1966</u>.

31. Telephone Interview with First Lieutenant William E. Black, on Friday 19 May 1967.

32. <u>Da Nang Press Briefing, 1100, 28 January 1966</u> pp. 4, 5, covering the period of Marine Corps action from 0600, 27 January-0600, 28 January 1966.

33. For details about Operation DOUBLE EAGLE see, Sgt Bob Bowen, "Operation Double Eagle I," <u>Leatherneck</u>, Vol. XLIX, No. 6, June 1966, pp. 26-29, and Sgt Bob Bowen, "Operation DOUBLE EAGLE II," <u>Leatherneck</u>, Vol. XLIX, No. 6, pp. 30-33, 81.

34. 3d Marine Division, <u>Command Chronology</u>, <u>February 1966</u> (S), p. 29.

35. III MAF, <u>Command Chronology</u>, <u>February 1966</u> (S), p. 20.

36. III MAF, <u>Command Chronology</u>, <u>February 1966</u> (S), p. 18.

37. III MAF, <u>Command Chronology</u>, <u>February 1966</u> (S), p. 20.

38. Cdr J. F. Dow, Letter, OP-345F, X57725, 10 November 1965, <u>Project HANDCLASP/Civic Action</u>. Commander Dow was the Naval Operations Coordinator for Project HANDCLASP in 1965.

39. Telephone Conversation with the Director, Project Handclasp, Cdr Arthur P. Ismay, U. S. Navy, on Monday 5 June 1967.

40. Interview with Col Don P. Wyckoff on Thursday 8 June 1967. Col Wyckoff was the Assistant Chief of Staff, G-3, 3d Marine Division in August 1965.

41. FMF Pac, <u>Professional Knowledge Gained from Operational Experience in Vietnam, January 1967</u>, pp. 42, 43. See also, FMFPac, <u>Professional Experience Gained from Operational Experience in Vietnam, October 1966</u>, pp. 1-3.

42. <u>Ibid</u>., p. 42.

43. 3d Marine Division, <u>Command Chronology</u>, <u>March 1966</u> (S), p. 19.

44. CG, III MAF, <u>County Fair Operations</u>, 7 August 1966. This document is a message addressed to CG, FMFPac (070332Z August 1966) and includes the pamphlet entitled, 9th Marines, <u>Operation County Fair</u>. The pamphlet states that "over twenty county fairs were held during July in villages throughout the three tactical areas" of III MAF.

45. FMFPac, <u>Professional Knowledge Gained from Operational Experience in Vietnam, October 1966</u>, pp. 53, 54.

46. <u>Ibid</u>., p. 53.

47. <u>Ibid</u>., p. 54.

48. Comparison of the material contained in Marine Corps Historical Reference Series, Number 21, <u>The United States Marines in Nicaragua</u>, Revised 1962, with the details of the intervention in Vietnam supported the view that the intensity and pervasiveness of the Vietnamese struggle rated it as a "different" experience.

49. See John Mecklin, "The Struggle to Rescue the People," <u>Fortune</u>, April 1967, pp. 126-139, 238-247, for an imaginative

yet sound analysis of the Viet Cong's method of "advance."

50. FMFPac, *Professional Knowledge Gained from Operational Experience in the Republic of Vietnam*, August 1966, p. 39.

51. FMFPac, *Tactical Trends and Training Tips*, January 1966, pp. 2, 3.

52. Marine Corps Bulletin 3480, 1 August 1966, Encl (2) *Civic Action Lessons Learned*, p. 4.

53. *Ibid.*, p. 5.

APPENDIX

Contents of CARE kits provided through
Reserve Civic Actions Fund for Vietnam

Elementary School Kit

Quantity	Item
2	Pen Points
1	Pen Holder
1	Ink Holder
*2	Notebooks (100 pages)
1	Ruler
*24	Ink Pellets
1	Slate
*2	Erasers
*4	Blotting Paper
*2	Pencils
*4	Pieces of Chalk
*1	Plastic bag to contain the kit

*Classroom Supply Kit Items
    For those students who need only the replacement components

Classroom Supply Kit

Quantity	Item
2	Notebook
24	Ink Pellets
2	Erasers
4	Blotting Paper
2	Pencils
1	Plastic Bag
1	Piece of Chalk

Sewing Kit

Quantity	Item
1	Scissors
1	Packet of Needles
1	Spool of Black Thread

Physical Education Kit

Quantity	Item
1	Soccer Ball
1	Volley Ball
1	Volley Ball Net

Textile Package

Quantity	Item
12 m	Black Rayon
1,600 m	Black Sewing Thread
75	Needles
0.75 kg	Laundry Soap
144	Black Plastic Buttons
1	Scissors

Midwifery Kit

Quantity	Item
1	Sponge Bowl
1	Stainless Steel Tray
1	Surgical Scissors
2	Forceps
2	Plastic Bottles
1	Packet of Safety Pins
18	Sterile Packets
1	Plastic Soap Container
2	Toilet Soap
1	Plastic Nail Brush
2	Hand Towel
1	Plastic Apron
1	Clear Vinyl Sheeting
1	Waterproof Bag

Blacksmith Kit

Quantity	Item
1	Bellow
1	Hacksaw Frame
12	12" Hacksaw Blades
1	Aluminum Ruler
1	Steel Tin Snip
1	Sledge Hammer
1	Square Hammer
1	Vice
1	12" Bastard File
1	12" 2nd Cut File
1	Half Round 2nd Cut File
1	Ballpeen Hammer
1	32" Tongs
1	Cold Chisel

Midwifery Replacement Kit

Quantity	Item
8 cakes	Soap
2 each	Hand Towels
2 each	Nail Brushes
2 each	Vinyl Plastic Aprons
18 each	Sterile Packets, each containing 2 umbilical tapes, 16" strand, one muslin binder 18" x 40", and one gauze pad, 3", 12 ply

Woodworking Kit

Quantity	Item
1	Ripsaw Blade
1	Crosscut Saw Blade
1	Claw Hammer
1	Steel Plane
1	Triangle File
1	5 Piece Chisel Set
1	12mm Drill Bit
1	16mm Drill Bit
1	Aluminum Ruler

SOURCE: Cooperative for American Relief Everywhere, Inc. 34 Ngo Nhiem, Saigon, Guidelines and Instructions, pp. 2-3.

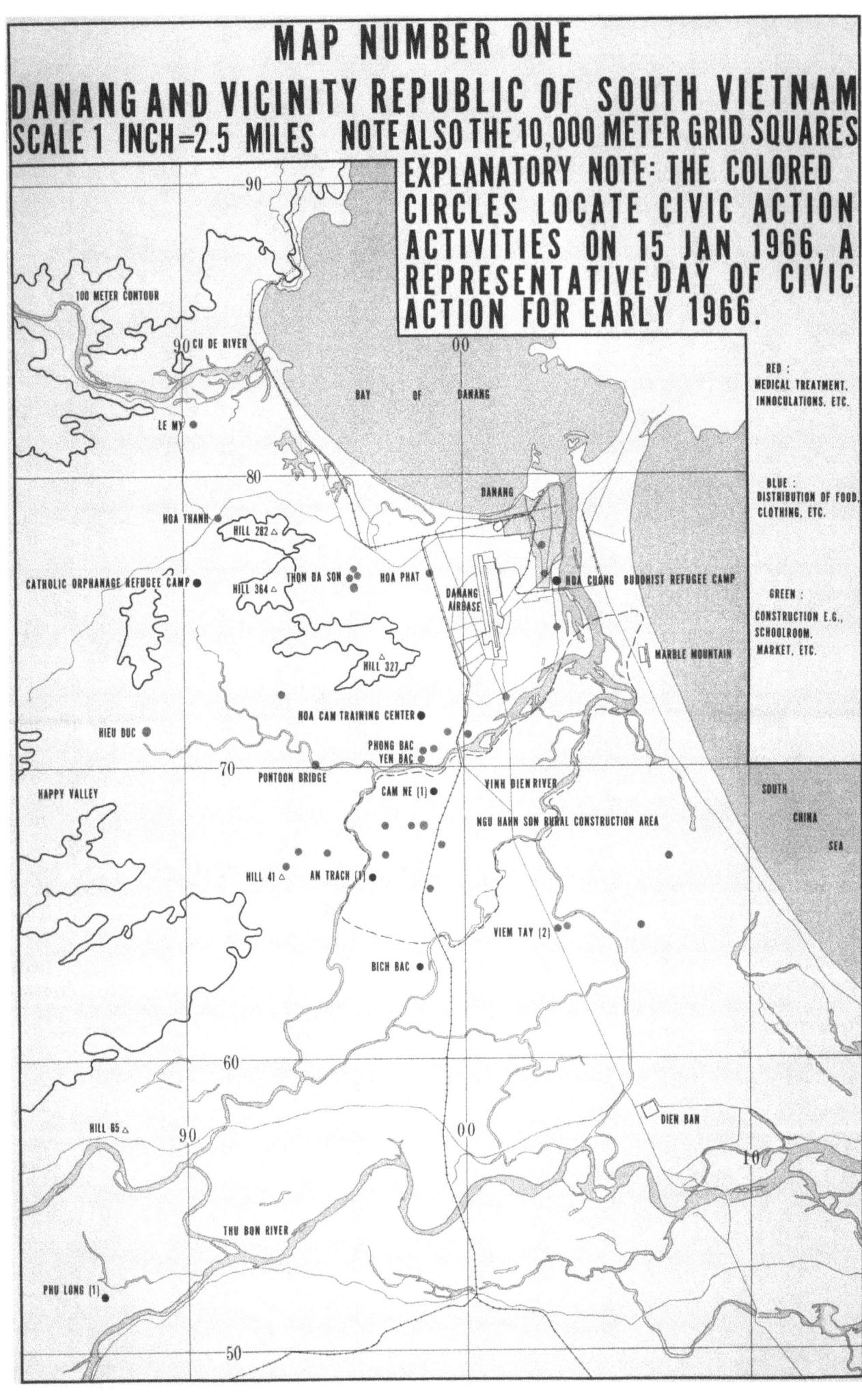

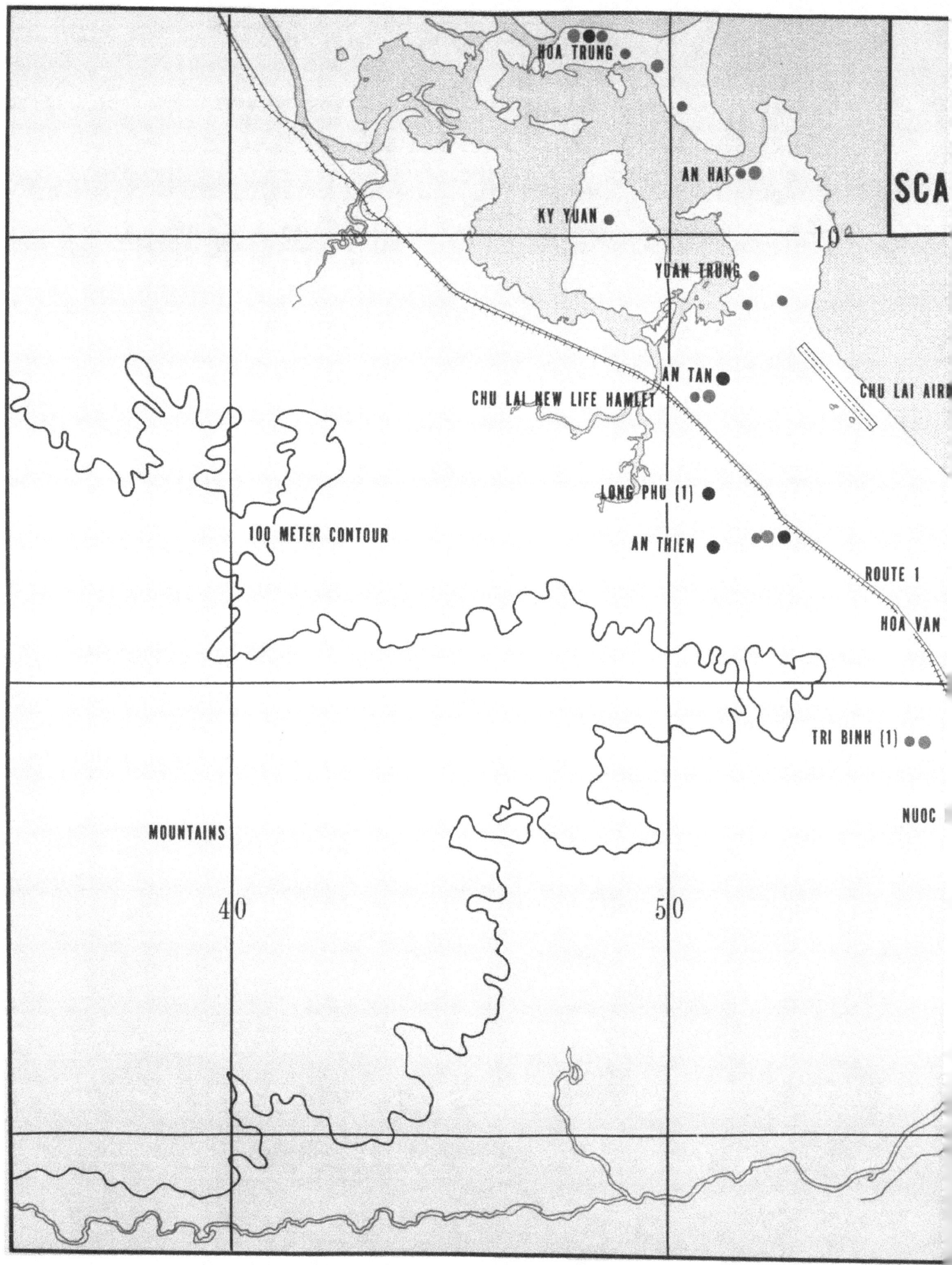

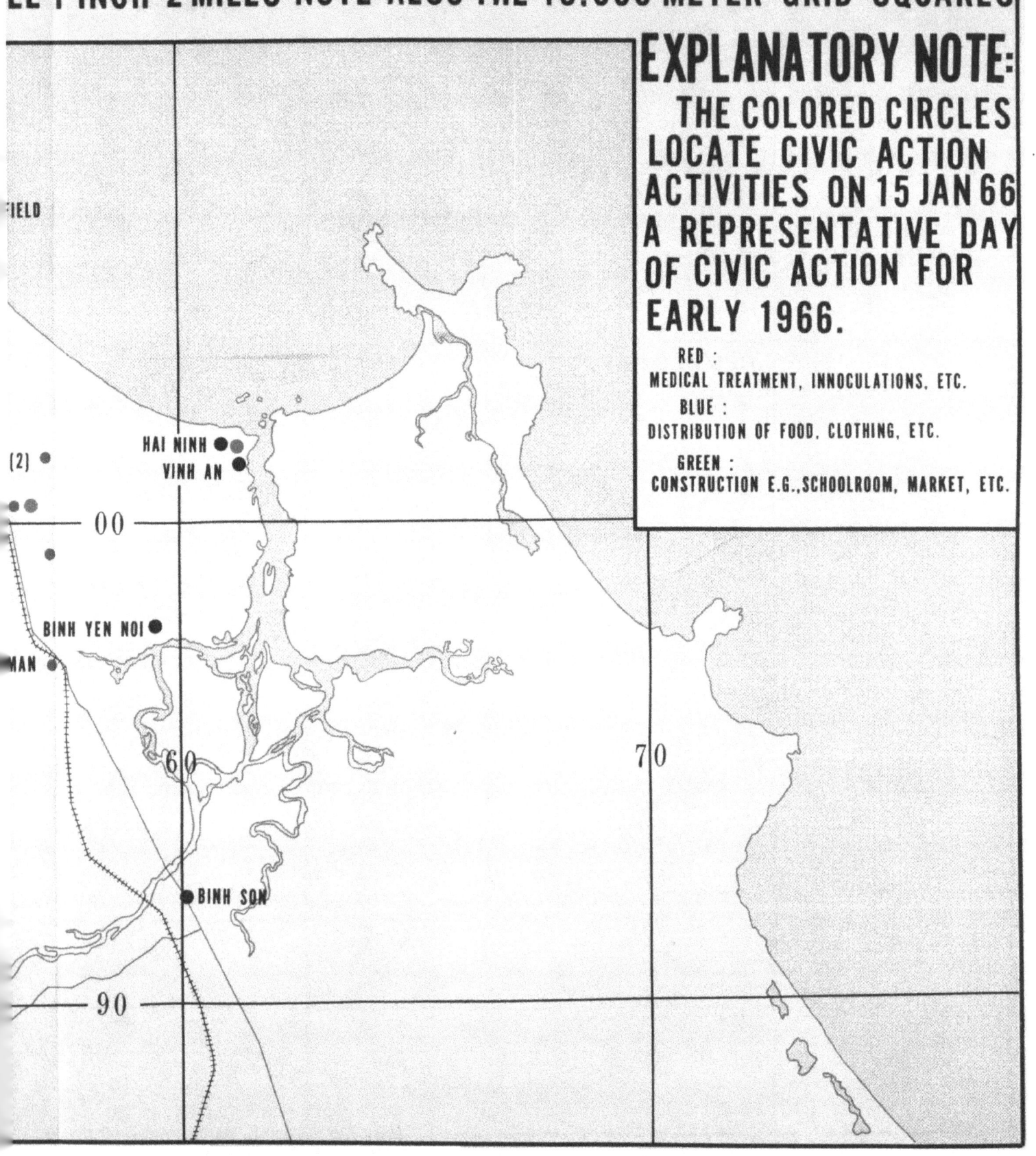

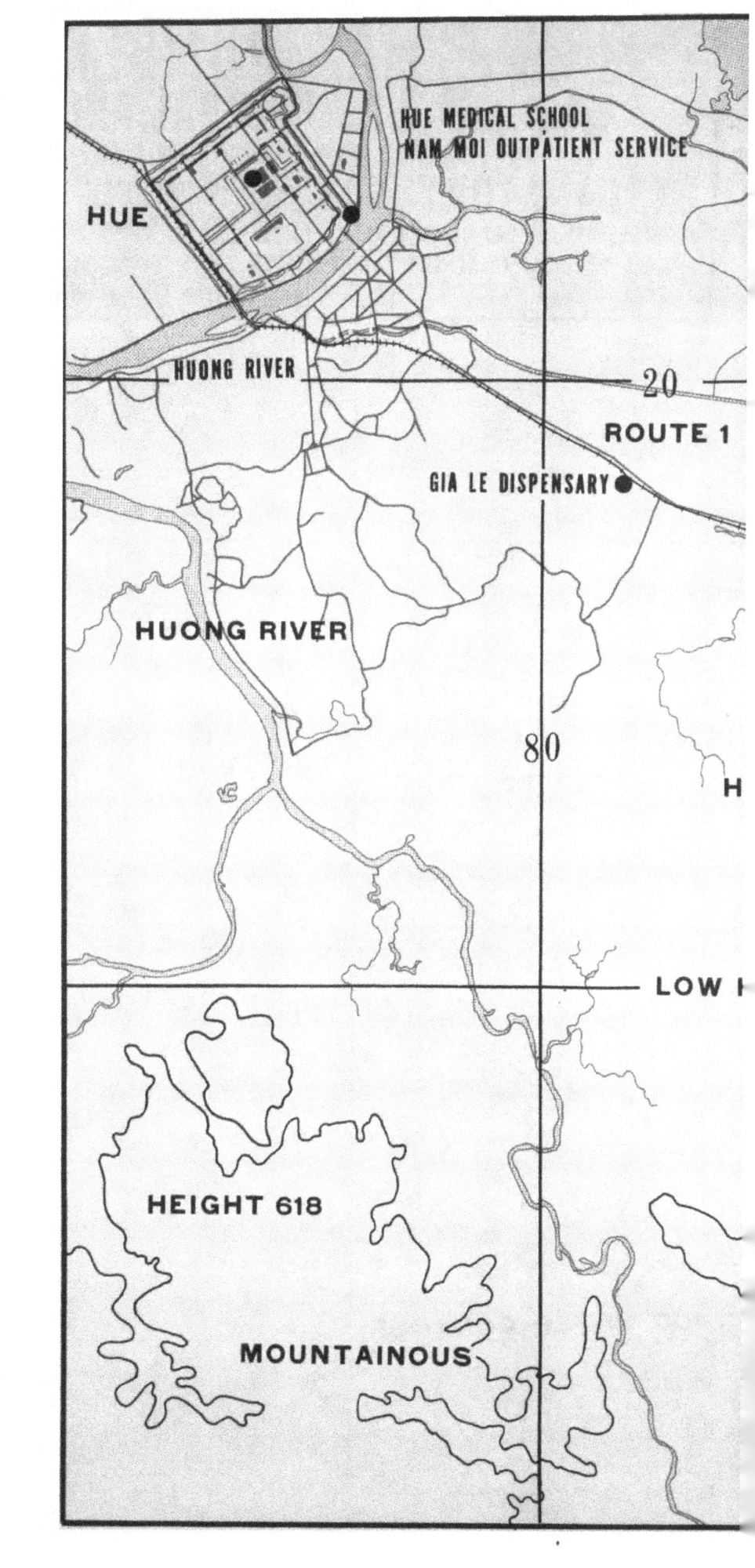

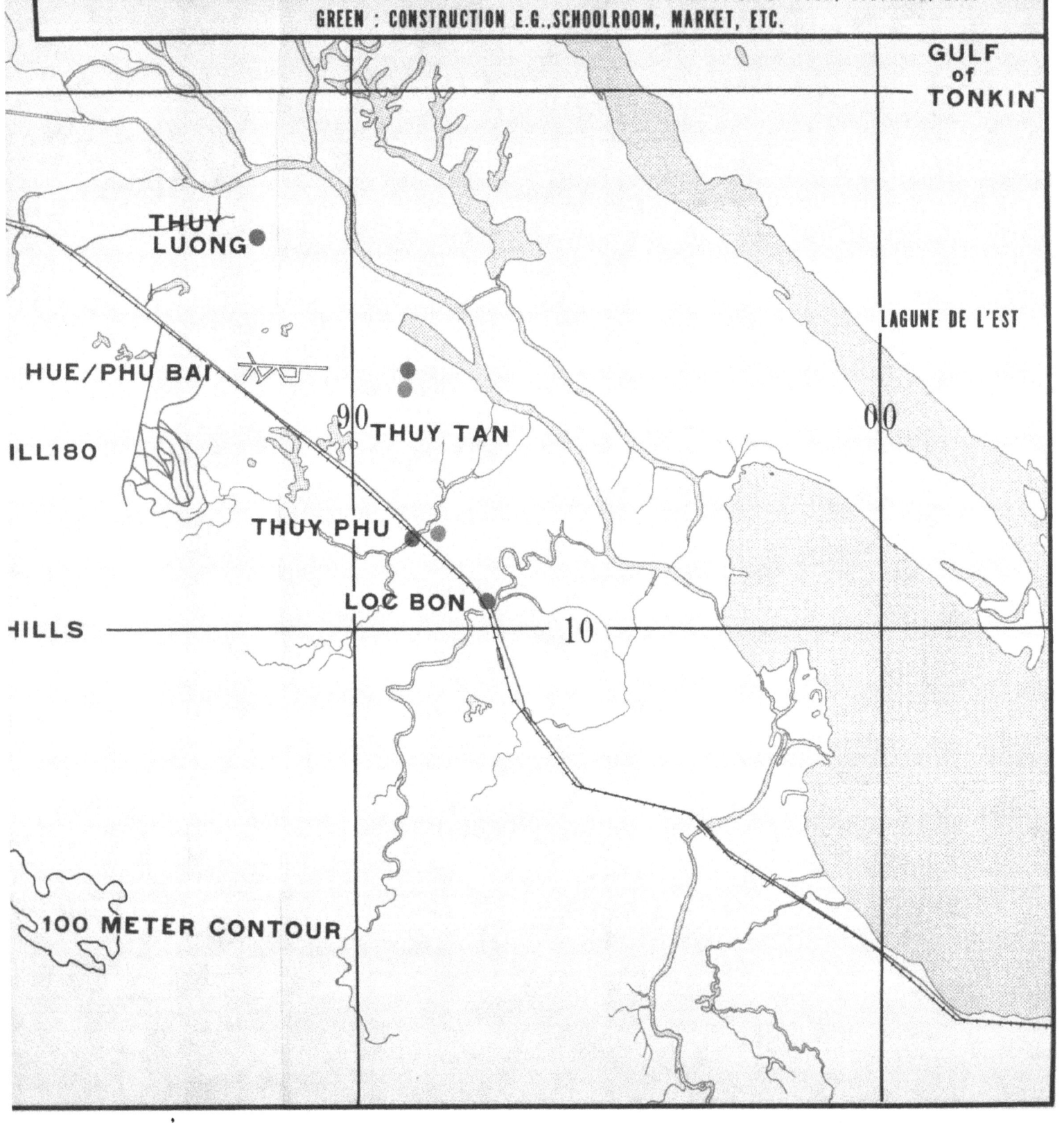

www.ingramcontent.com/pod-product-compliance
Lightning Source LLC
Chambersburg PA
CBHW080516110426
42742CB00017B/3130